Here's what folks are saying about Holy Wow!

"When I sit to read *Holy Wow!*, I feel like I'm sitting with a dear friend who is showing me a new way to look at my existence." ~ **Deb B.**

"This book is a gift and a wonderful read! *Holy Wow!* takes us along on one woman's life long exploration of her own spirituality, along the way giving us a warm and very informative tour of that same territory in ourselves. A User's Manual. Lots of fun and highly recommended." ~ **Mitch E.**

"*Holy Wow! The Blessing Is Being Here* is unlike any other book about meditation I have ever read and I loved every minute of it! A profound message shines out from a background of wry humor and wit. This book is a treasure of hilarious insights and practical ways of coping with being in our Earth Suits." ~ **Judy H.**

"Warm, witty and wise. I just finished *Holy Wow! Volume I*. And I will read it again. Dana has a charming way of imparting useful, relevant advice. Thank you so much for sharing this with me and all our fellow travelers!" ~ **Nancy K.**

"*Holy Wow!* is a contemporary scripture! A Masterpiece. It makes clear esoteric metaphysical concepts via a lovingly guided, delightful journey. Each chapter has a unique ambiance.

"I highly recommend this extraordinary book to both neophyte and veteran students of metaphysics. All readers will come away from *Holy Wow!* with a clear, fresh awareness of everything they've ever wanted to know about life. **~ Karen M.**

"This spiritual journey was masterfully written. It is an easy read, witty, comedic, insightful and an eye opener. With wisdom expressed in so many areas. The concept that humans operate with three bodies, the physical, emotional, and mental in our human host experience is very enlightening. There are many life lessons to be gained by reading this book. One that resonated for me: "Your life is about what you give your attention to." There is a wealth of information enclosed in these pages – Enjoy." **~ Cathy S.**

"Dana St. Claire has done a fabulous job expressing herself in this book. I do recommend the audio version if you want to catch Dana's true "flair!" You can really feel the personality behind the clever writing when you hear her delicious voice!!" **~ Elizabeth B.**

"You need to read Dana St. Claire's *Holy Wow!* right away. You may not know this yet, but that's exactly why you need to read it right away.

"Dana writes with genuine wit, humor and compassion as she guides us toward a deeper understanding of our place in the universe. She doesn't tell us how to achieve "enlightenment." Instead, she provides valuable tools that help us figure it out for ourselves. Most important, Dana acknowledges that the path is different for everyone, and there isn't one "right" way to achieve higher consciousness and self-awareness.

"*Holy Wow!* would be a great book to help you navigate the journey of life at any time. In the times we're currently living through, it's a necessary and vital read. The book is really tremendous and filled with many "aha" moments, and more than a few laughs of recognition. Can't wait for *Volume II* to see what happens next!" ~ **Mark W.**

Holy Wow!

Holy Wow!

The HazMat Variety Show

Volume III

Dana St. Claire

© 2021 by Maylaigh Media

All rights reserved. No part of this book may be reproduced or transmitted in any form or by any means, electronic or mechanical, including photocopying, recording, or by any information storage and retrieval system, except in the case of brief quotations embodied in critical articles and reviews, without prior written permission of the publisher.

Although the author and publisher have made every effort to ensure the accuracy and completeness of information contained in this book, we assume no responsibility for errors, inaccuracies, omissions, or any inconsistency herein.

ISBN Paperback: 978-1-7331059-6-5
ISBN eBook: 978-1-7331059-8-9
ISBN Audio: 978-1-7331059-7-2

Cover artwork: Miladinka Milic
Interior design: Ghislain Viau

I dedicate this book to my remarkable daughter, Lyla.
My role model for embracing Life.
Thanks, Darlin', for ALL your insight and encouragement.
I am where I am because of you.

And this book is dedicated to You, my kind Reader.
I celebrate your choice to incarnate human.
Value your Life.
Value the contribution you are to our world.

As you explore and radiate your Light,
you contribute to the awakening of each Life you touch.

Thank You for that.

Appetizers

Reading *Holy Wow!* is your opportunity to look at the living of your perplexing… yet fascinating… human Life from a different perspective.

Thanks for checking it out.

Here are some useful tips and info… with a little backstory.

I have been "on the verge of writing a book" since my early 20s… in the early '70s. In 2016/17, following 5 successful hypnotherapy sessions… I finally wrote "my book." Turns out… after such a rich and long gestation… I had plenty to say. As originally written, *Holy Wow!* is one very long book… with 13 chapters. Early in my Adventures In Publishing… book publishing professionals suggested

I divide *Holy Wow!* into 3 volumes. Initially, I resisted. I liked *Holy Wow!* just the way it was. But you know, it didn't take me long to see the wisdom in their advice. Now, *Holy Wow!* is indeed divided into 3 volumes. *Volume I* contains chapters 1-5. *Volume II* covers chapters 6-9. In *Volume III*, you will find chapters 10-13.

This book you are perusing… *Volume III* = the final 4 chapters of the original manuscript. If you've read *Volumes I* and/or *II*… *Volume III* has you moving along in a fun and familiar direction. *Volumes I* and *II* do contain useful backstory and additional handy information. However, if you're not able to lay your eyes on *Volumes I* and *II* to read first… go ahead and read *Volume III*. You will have an informative and uplifting experience. It'll work for you.

The subtitle of *Volume III* is *The HazMat Variety Show*. The HazMat designation refers to the hazardous mental and emotional reactive materials activated on Planet Earth. Rage. Vengeance. Hatred. Greed. Each and all… corrosive and toxic. Of course there are also the risky physical elements… explosives… radioactivity… poisons. If not handled with the necessary precaution protocols… all of these various toxic materials… vengeance and hatred… explosives and poison… pose a danger to the living of human Life. The Variety Show aspect speaks for itself. On Planet Earth, there is plenty of variety. Plenty of hazardous materials. Plenty of show.

Appetizers

They don't call Earth "The Planet of Paradox" for nothin'.

Volume III beginning, as it does, with what was originally Chapter 10… is 2/3 into the manuscript as it was originally written. You can easily imagine those first 9 chapters (now in *Volumes I* and *II*) rolled out numerous foundational themes, elements, and information. Written in the process of that developing context… Chapter 10 rocks some far-ranging insightful material.

The voice of your Interpretorium Tour Guide welcomes you as *Volume III* begins. The Interpretorium is where pre-incarnate beings go for Orientation… preparing for their upcoming incarnate adventure… Human On Planet Earth. This Orientation venue is called The Interpretorium to honor this fact: As you are human, your interpretations weave the fabric of your Life. The way you *interpret* input and issues renders the texture of your beliefs. Beliefs about yourself… your talents and limitations. About others… frustrations and fascinations. Beliefs about your Life… your opportunities and challenges.

As you interpret… each and every thing… so do you believe. Your interpretations are the bedrock of your personal truth. Your version of all that is happening to you. Your story of what this human incarnation of yours is all about. Gross or groovy.

During Orientation, each pre-incarnate being inhabits their own Tri-Body Bio Energy Simulator... their B.E. Suit. This simulator allows them to experience the commotion of physical, emotional, and mental reality... in "real time." Just like on Planet Earth. This simulated reality is enhanced by the state-of-the-art Realizmotron Scenario Generator... creating Life-like dioramas and authentic incidents. During their time in The Interpretorium, these pre-incarnate beings have the opportunity to explore and inhabit a cornucopia of upcoming human circumstances and capabilities.

After those hypnotherapy sessions... as I began writing "my book" in earnest... out came something I did not consider before. Surprise!

It had never occurred to me to write about *my* Life. My story. My foibles and fascinations. How I began meditating... what I did with it. Different aspects of my Life unfolding... realizations... obstacle illusions... Life patterns. Guiding Women's Spirit Circles. Singing. Chanting. Raising children... meeting Scott... teaching meditation. Who'd want to know about that?

Yet, as I sat to write Chapter 1... that is exactly what came pouring out.

In the 13 chapters of *Holy Wow!*... all of the even-numbered chapters take place as pre-incarnate beings participate in Orientation at The Interpretorium. All of

Appetizers

the odd-numbered chapters are my story... a potpourri of my Life experiences. How this all came about.

Reading the odd numbered chapters in *Volume III*... you will see reference to "The Nature of The Soul." This is an esoteric training program I studied extensively in my early 20s. Here I learned to teach meditation. Assimilating this deep spiritual training set my feet firmly upon my path in this incarnation. Lucky me to "stumble into it" at such a young age.

You will also read about the other significant training I received in my early 20s... the Life-clarifying teachings of Tibetan Buddhism. The grace of these practices integrated into the terrain of my inner world as I lived at Nyingma Institute... in the foothills of Berkeley, California.

You will find reference to "Your Etheric Sconce." This "container" is the very foundation of your current human incarnate instrument. It is an energy sheath woven from the fabric of past incarnate traumas and realizations. Attitudes. Obstacles. Likelihoods. Dharma. The deep, eternal nature of your etheric mechanism contains the karmic roadmap... the attractions and distractions... of your current incarnate Life.

You'll meet a Recent Returnee... fresh from her most recent incarnation on Planet Earth. As in *Volume II*... she continues sharing wisdom gleaned... tips and insights... for embracing your upcoming bold, bodacious human brouhaha. As our session ended in *Volume II* ... she encouraged Orientation attendees to check out the latest sexosity seminar... "Sexness Rocks." In *Volume III*, conversation turns to kudos for the presenters' creativity as they offer pointers and encourage exploring the physical body's sensual pleasures thru Tantric practices. Practices which consciously include Higher Light Awareness in the arousal mix.

Sexness = ever humanity's dilemma. Ever humanity's delight.

In *Volume III*, our Recent Returnee conveys her recent human awareness notes in the realm of forgiveness. She prompts incarnating beings to remember... forgiveness is of far greater advantage to the forgiver than it is to the forgiven. Forgiveness releases you. The human brain's neuroplasticity offers pre-packaged hardware with all the agility and resilience required for forgiveness. She counsels these pre-incarnate beings... as you are established in your human instrument... forgiveness is a practice... a self-training. Like exercising your gratitude muscle. The forgiver wins.

She includes valuable insight into raising children with attentive kindness. Along with her perceptive commentary on parenting with loving awareness... she also offers a tool for an adult to access and heal childhood trauma and misrelationship. Allowing repurposing of those energies long snared there.

Understanding the true wisdom of forgiveness… equipt with enriching parenting skills… embracing the grace of vibrant sexuality… these all have a profound impact on how gratifying… how luminous… this upcoming human incarnation will be.

With the help of Realizmotron's Authentic Dioramas… Orientation participants explore the vast and various locales where humans can incarnate on Planet Earth. From the Poles to the Equator and back again.

Holy Wow! Volume III explores seminal teachings of the Buddha… one of the great World Teachers. Buddha advised… inhabit the middle way between the extremes of Life. He also insightfully declared… "Your worst enemy cannot harm you as much as your own unguarded thoughts." Tame the wild stallion of your mind. Free yourself from self-induced afflictions which arise from wrong thought… from wrong perception. Buddha's teachings are about releasing your self from suffering. This is the ultimate freedom while you are incarnate human.

Open yourself to receive the lessons of this Life… both the miraculous and the mundane. Your enlightened knowledge benefits all Humankind.

Your Orientation Tour Guide also offers perception into the benefits of meditating as an incarnate human. Meditation reveals yourself to you. The unnecessary veil of self-reproach is lifted. You open to the grace of your inner healing process. Leading you to a finer degree of self-awareness and self-compassion. Leading you to a finer degree of compassion toward others. And toward this Life we are all living.

In Volume III, we also deepen our exploration and understanding of Maylaigh... The Love That Heals. Ahhh... The Love That *Heals*. Deepen into *that* Love. Relax the frightened vigilance of your emotions. The fabrication of self-incited drama evaporates. Realization of the spacious grace of The Love That Heals grants limitless understanding. Peace. Self-kindness. Loving participation in your Life. Generosity of Spirit prevails.

Looking at the Table of Contents here in *Volume III*... you will see the original chapter numbering has been retained. There's a reason for this. Among a variety of topics in Chapter 13, I write about triskaidekaphobia ... the fear of the number 13. Doesn't it seem the "natural flow" would be askew if you read about triskaidekaphobia in Chapter 4... which the original Chapter 13 is now in *Volume III*? Exactly!

To demark the original chapter numbering in the Table of Contents... *Chapter One* is written in text above the numeral " <u>10</u> "... bold, underlined and in quote marks. *Chapter Two* is written above the numeral " <u>11</u> ". And so on. ("10" and "11" are the original chapter numbers.) Thus… chapter numbering retained.

Before you start Chapter One (aka Chapter "10") you will see "Thanks For Riding Along With Me." Here I share some of my stylistic tendencies… like ('…')… altho and thru… additional unique spelling choices… my use of numerals. This same commentary is at the beginning of *Volumes I* and *II*. If you read "Thanks For Riding Along With Me" in *Volume I* or *II*, you don't need to read it again. If you're starting here with *Volume III*, you'll want to give it a look. "Thanks For Riding Along With Me" explains a few things.

Two more pieces of pertinent info: I capitalize the word "Life" out of respect… for Life. And… thru-out *Holy Wow!* you will see reference to us being "Spirit living a human experience." Because we are.

When you are busy being human… cruising around in your physical, emotional, mental expression… *you* are so much more than the sum of your parts. So. Much. More.

There is *so much more* we can live and give. So much more we can each perceive. Feel. Realize. Be.

Focus your energy… your attention… on being the best you. Don't waste your precious human Life fussing about "others." Apply your bodacious Life energies to become the most loving, understanding you. The most contributing you. The most helpful you.

Incredible elements of awareness and authenticity are available to us humans. Every one. You are here on this zany blue-green planet to live your Life effectively. To live an effective, contributing Life.

We are all in this together… each a droplet of water in the ocean of Life. As you shine your Light of caring and kindness… showing up in your Life present and engaged… you remind others they are capable of doing the same.

>Your energies… your Life expression…
>are much appreciated.

Table of Contents

Thanks for Riding Along with Me

Page 1

Chapter One
" <u>10</u> "
**The Ever-Exhilarating Bliss
of Pure Light Consciousness**

"Shower the people you love with love."

Page 5

Chapter Two
" <u>11</u> "
Maylaigh: The Love That Heals

"I was reaching for Love. Where did all this not-Love come from?!"

Page 79

Chapter Three
" <u>12</u> "
The HazMat Variety Show

"I'll take Door #2, Johnny."

Page 131

Chapter Four
" <u>13</u> "
Dare To Take The Step
*"Or... attitude being everything...
you could say, here's where the fun begins."*
Page 209

Acknowledgments
Page 275

About the Author
Page 279

Thanks for Riding Along with Me

Okay, so right here at the get-go, I am going to tell you something about my writing style. I like words. And I like playing with them. I don't want you to think my wonderful book editor didn't catch my stylistic tendencies. Rather, she chose to let my writing be my writing. Which I hugely appreciate.

Let's start with '…'. You will learn as you read *Holy Wow!* that this book had an incredibly long gestation period. As it finally started tumbling out, it came with '…'. A breath, a beat, a moment. If using '…' was finally how things were going to get going… who was I to resist? This '…' worked well for me. And it kept working. Naturally, I hope it works well for you, too.

Over the 4 decades as *Holy Wow!* gestated, I did, of course, write other things. When I wrote, I used "tho" for "though" and "thru" for "through"… which quite naturally led to "altho" and "thru-out." When my editor, Pam, first read my Holy Wow! manuscript, she pointed out that I was using "texting language." She expressed concern that some readers might criticize my choices and think less of my work because of such abbreviations… such casual language. As I have used these spellings my entire adult Life… I pointed out that texting just finally caught up with me. I don't mean to be vexing… this is just the way I write.

I totally understand the proper and professional… and I want you to know that Pam is both. It's me that feels odd seeing "tho" and "thru" completely spelled out in my writing. That doesn't look like me. I realize those spellings are considered by some to be text shorthand. To me… they are just the more sensible way to spell those words.

On to another thing or 2. Did you know that humans devised and used numbers centuries before letters were invented? This development of numbers, counting, and recording systems was humanity's first long-distance communication tool, having a profound effect on the ability to share knowledge, transmit information and thrive. I am intrigued by this historical significance of numbers. Giving a shout out to numbers… in my writing, I use the actual numeral to indicate numbers. (Except in the rare case when a number starts a sentence… then, I spell the word rather than using the number symbol.)

I use the word "grok" to mean "deeply understand." I also use the word "connexion" to indicate ever-so-much more connected that a mere connection. Here and there I use "yeah" as an informal "yes"… not to mean "yay." You will also find the occasional unique spelling of a word, and capitalizations that indicate certain Orientation Programs and Certifications. Now and again, in the midst of a sentence, you will come across an " = " sign. As in… "This ability to have a chuckle = a most sanity-producing maneuver as you are busy being human."

There is additional creative spelling and word usage… "intellecting" or "thinkery," for instance… which, to me, are self-explanatory. The words "equipt" or "spoilt" you may recognize as the British spelling. I've always liked them spelled that way. Words are tricky little comprehension packets. You will come across "cognent," which can be seen as a blend of "cogent" and "cognitive." I use "cognent" to describe the beings who are not in incarnation, yet. And "incarnant" to describe the beings who are.

I share this with you, Dear Reader, to say… these writing nuances are neither mistakes nor oddities. They are the creative choices that make *Holy Wow!* the experience it is. I write this to thank you for riding along with me and for easing into my stylistic ways. Now, let's have some fun!

CHAPTER ONE

" <u>10</u> "

The Ever-Exhilarating Bliss of Pure Light Consciousness

"Shower the people you love with love."

Well, look at you! Here you are… preparing to Incarnate Human On Planet Earth… marinating in an invigorating dose of All that means.

I know you are well aware… that "All" is *A Lot* of Everything!

As your Orientation Moment continues… it is my pleasure to welcome you back to The Interpretorium. Our focus here is to prepare you… somewhat… for this deep dive you are taking into "The Zaniness of Being Human." (And *All* that means.) As we consider Earthtone Humanness… there really isn't a better way to put it. "Zany" fills the bill. Perusing human terminology… we find "zany" defined as "being comical or ludicrous because of incongruity or strangeness, a person given to extravagant or outlandish, eccentric behavior."

Recalling your past incarnate experiences, you undoubtedly remember… humans of Earth are indeed a pretty "eccentric" bunch… more than a little "outlandish." Definitely unique.

Truth be told… each incarnant human lives in their own individual bubble. On their own private planet. Each human travels their own remarkable terrain. With their own distinct inner attunements, nuanced outer coordinates and beguiling personal expression. Each individual human is wired to determine… "What does *this* mean?" "What's *that* about?" "How is this all going to affect *me*?" Increasing the juiciness factor… each incarnate human arrives with their own entourage. Their own distinctive cast of fascinating characters, comrades and cohorts they will carry on with thru different Life escapades.

Oh, those wily humans. Twisted. Insecure. Divine.

Keep in mind… each human incarnates on Planet Earth for their own array of vast and various reasons and purposes.

The Ever-Exhilarating Bliss of Pure Light Consciousness

Some humans incarnate to be strong, gifted athletes. Some to be bright, inquisitive scholars or scientists. Some to be store clerks, bank tellers or machinery operators. Some men are ballet dancers. Some women are welders. There are some humans who incarnate to be good parents. And some who have no intention of having children.

Each person so completely unique. With so many different choices. Actors, athletes and acrobats. Politicians, poets and personal trainers. Influencers. Home makers, herdsmen and fry cooks. A vast array of different ways of doing. A vast array of different ways of being.

Many humans get snagged… "They're doing it wrong!" (Whoever "they" are.) "They should think and believe as I do." "They should be more like *I* think they should be." No, actually… they shouldn't. You go to Planet Earth to be you. The best "you" you can be. They go to Planet Earth to be them. Their best selfs. An endeavor they're working on… whether they do it your way, or not.

Here's a worthwhile suggestion… as you are being human… rather than criticizing others because they don't think and believe "like me"… focus your energy and attention on being the best you. The most loving, understanding you. The most contributing you. The most helpful you.

Humans seem compelled to criticize. It's just so easy. So easy to point out all the things they see as wrong. Humans spend a lot of their precious time doing that. Criticizing. It's the easy way. The lazy way. "I don't have to be a better me... I'll just criticize and belittle people or things I don't understand. Then I'll feel better about myself." Really? Actually... it doesn't work that way.

I know, sitting here in cognitive reality... you're thinking, "Of course I'm going to Planet Earth to be the best me I can be!" Yes, that is the most efficient, most effective way to do it. But alas... passing thru those wily etheric veils... the calcifying mind control of your early years... the false beliefs that keep you frightened, constricted. Each and every one... so beguiling. So delusional. So self-limiting.

In our last Orientation session, as we focused on "Your Human Apparatus Does Life on Planet Earth"... I'm sure you found both substance and value as our Recent Returnee shared insights and realizations gleaned from her most recent Planet Earth incarnation. Her presentation is a fine example of our most helpful Team Interpretorium efforts... priming your pump for your upcoming gig on that ever-engaging Planet of Paradox.

As her presentation drew to a close, she provided this most useful piece of information:

> "When you are busy being human... cruising around in your physical, emotional, mental expression...

you are so much more than the sum of your parts.

So. Much. More."

As you are an incarnate human, you are not just your hustle and bustle… your thinkery and perceptions… your upsets and delights… your endeavors and pursuits. There is more to you than that.

Let us consider the majestic mountains of Planet Earth. In their entirety… their bearing and demeanor are so much more than their dirt, rocks and vegetation. Their parts are just their parts. Their totality is… magnificent.

Ditto you.

As an incarnate human, you are so much more than your ideas and perceptions… your overthink and insecurities… your busyness and behaviors.

There is an astonishing brilliance about you.

The spark of Spirit animates you… vitalizing your Life. Shining thru your eyes… thru your touch… thru the tone of your voice and the words that you choose. Thru your work, your play, your creative expression.

Incarnating human on Planet Earth, you are, indeed Spirit living a human experience. Altho, I gotta say… immersed within It All… this truth is easy to lose sight of.

Oh, that unpredictable cauldron of human experience! Engrossed in your mighty sweat and swirl… there you are…

harassed by your own free will, attitudes and appetites. Your own inner feelings of inadequacy and general disappointment. Is *this* all there is?!

I know. I know. As you sit here in the bliss of pure cognizant reality... I hear you thinking, "But being human is such fun! It'll be so groovy! I'll have 5 delectable senses to experience Life! I'll not only see and touch the world around me... I'll be able to taste it, too! I'll suit up in a tri-body instrument! Not just brawn and brain. I'll be immersed in a vast and wide emotional nature which will be my clear, light-reflective surface for the Light of the Soul. So cool. It can't get any better than that. I can hardly wait!"

Uh... yeah. Hang on a minute. Now I don't want to ick your wow. But, I gotta tell you... all this groovyness you're anticipating... uhhh. Well, let's just say... incarnate Life on Earth does not play out as clear and bodacious as you may be envisioning while you sit here in the pure cognizant reality of The Interpretorium.

Remember... as you are incarnate human... you steep like a tea bag in the strong, scalding brew of the engaging interplay of "All that is being human" cruising thru the intersection of "All Life has to offer." There are unexpected twists of perception... sharp curves... bumps in the road. Blisters and bunions of human reality you truly are not able to anticipate before you get there.

The Ever-Exhilarating Bliss of Pure Light Consciousness

Sitting here now, you have no way to foresee the struggles and gripes... the exploits and wonders... the commotion... your upcoming incarnation has in store for you. The sheer magnitude of nuance and predicament is stunning. You may indeed have your colored streamers flying... your crash helmets more-or-less secure... hanging on as the propulsion of Life overtakes you. Saturates you. Thrusts you along your trajectory. Whoa baby... hang on! You could be in for a bumpy ride.

Our endeavor here at Team Interpretorium? We're your Cosmic Tour Guides... striving to prep you for riding the rodeo. By giving you insights and scenarios... perceptions and acumen... which will, hopefully, smooth some of the rougher edges. We suit you up with a saddle and reins... likely even chaps and stirrups... as you head on out there. Riding The Rodeo of Life.

As spoken in Planet Earth vernacular... "Choose wisely, Grasshopper."

And take a *deep* breath.

Does anyone have any questions? You may recall... a question is you putting into words something you are wondering about. No questions? Alrighty then. Moving on.

When our last session came to a close, our Recent Returnee encouraged you to check out the Sexness Rocks Seminar. Were you there? Did you take notes?

As our Recent Returnee mentioned, this is the first time we've combined "Awash in Estrogen" and "Testosterone: Hard Profile" into one sexosity seminar. Which, of course, is such a good idea. Keeping in mind... one doesn't get far without the other. It's all about rockin' that interplay.

The timing of the seminar was excellent. I'm sure you found a lot of valuable information among the realistic demonstrations and graphic discourse. Don't those presenters do an excellent job!? I saw our Recent Returnee stayed after the seminar to answer your questions about current Earthtone sexuality.

You will notice as you are being human on Planet Earth... for many, many humans... both the testosterone-laden units and many of the estrogen-infused components... sexness is at the forefront... of their thoughts... their fantasies... and their interactions.

As the Sexness Rocks Seminar demonstrated... these human thoughts... fantasies... sexual interactions... reside in a wide spectrum of both activity and artifice. Some degrees of human sexual experience can be hard core... "x-rated," as humans call it. Exposing oneself to the excitement... the arousal... of explicit description and display of sex organs. Graphic activity. Vivid. Intense.

Yet, as you just learned... intense and penetrating is not the *only* way to fly. Also included in this multi-layered sexosity spectrum... many humans find libido fascination in softer, sweeter stimulation. More aesthetic... artistic... emotional. Feelings... exchange... interplay. "Play" being the operative word. The blessed energy of connexion. The excitation of sensuality. Sweet embellishments. Special treats. Revealing clothing. Toys. The strategic licking off of whipped cream... warm honey... chocolate sauce.

The presenters serve you well as they encourage exploring the body's sensual pleasures thru Tantric practices... consciously including Higher Light Awareness in the arousal mix. The buoyant mind. Heart-nourishing interaction. Sweet physical delight. Which will or will not lead to actual sexual activity. Tantra. Opening to the erotic and titillating. Playing with the Light.

So many gratifying variations. Succumbing to the rough-riding and pornographic = not necessarily a requirement.

The mid-20th century brought a fascinating development in human sexosity. Some call it liberating. Manipulating synthetic (human-made) progesterone and estrogen hormones led to the development of a highly effective form of reversible birth control. The pill. This chemical maneuvering brought a massive change in the tantalizing tango between women and men. The sexual revolution. Humans can now frolic and play without persistent concern about the production of offspring.

Liberating, indeed. Certainly different from previous centuries of copulation. Not really "better" or "worse." Definitely different.

Finding a partner who likes to play sex the same way you do. Exquisite. "She likes to ride... he likes to be ridden." Good times. The best.

Drawing the Light of Spirit into sex play only enhances the Wow!

Depending on where you incarnate... you may find a surprising number of adult humans believe they should have some say in the way other adult humans experience their sexness. In the throes of judgement... they often demonstrate a flurry of fury. Really? One can't help but think... who are *they* to harshly judge others? How is it they believe they're entitled to insert themselves in such intimate matters? Despite their strong judgments and pointed opinions... you will find there is, in fact, no "right" or "wrong" way to explore your sexuality.

Employing here another human colloquialism... "Whatever floats your boat."

In the context of this vast, human interplay between testosterone and estrogen... you'll hear it said on Planet Earth... men give love to get sex... women give sex to get love. Emotional fulfillment and sexual gratification... eternally entwined. Relationship... dilemma and delight.

Humans are basically unaware… those biochemical hormones are the ones who call the shots on Planet Earth. Estrogen and testosterone are 2 of The Really Big Players. Captains of Team Reproduction. Make more Game pieces! In the midst of all they instigate… and all that transpires between them… these 2 hormones are recognized as the big movers and shakers on that blue-green orb.

Here we have an additional opportunity to grok humans in their role as action figures. Pump them full of hormones and watch them rollick and roll! Always keeping in perspective the sustaining interest the "higher realms" have in the continuation of each species. Reproduction of viable units. Keep those game pieces comin'.

Must keep The Game afoot.

The Game don't play without them game pieces. We need those players playing. And reproducing.

The brilliant decision to make human reproductive activity alluring… "sexy"… "hot"… guarantees keeping them humans enthusiastically engaged in this activity of furthering the species. You're not going to find many folks giving a moment's thought to "continuation of the species" as they are looking for, or engaging in, sex.

And there it is! The beauty of the whole "make sex hot" strategy. It works.

As in the Animal Kingdom... many times it is the human male... responding to rushing testosterone... who initiates copulation. Male animals are actually more gripped by their reproductive urges than male humans. The reflexive activity of animals... free from any smidge of intellectual reasoning... seasoning... or redirecting... has the male of the species completely at the mercy of his own estrus. Instinctual urges. Pheromones. Victimized by his own unrelenting urge to rut. "Where are they!? Where's them females!?"

Oh, yoo-hoo. Here she is. The female of the species. Awash in her own instinctual bio-chemicals... the female animal, usually swept away in the intensity of the moment, is more than willing to comply. Occasionally, she resists. That doesn't last long. The reflexive power of instinct. The force of those bio-chemicals. With very little wiggle room for holding out... she succumbs

Yet... animal coitus is a far cry from human sex play. Copulation... as it plays out in the animal world is... different. Abrupt. The humongous urges to reproduce in the animal kingdom... arrive in the company of many alluring scents and odors built right into the process. Sniff... sniff. "Whoa! That's it! Gotta get me some females!!"

One noteworthy difference between male animals and male humans... the male of the animal species spends significantly more time fighting other males... defending his right to his females... than he spends in the actual act of copulating with his females. A quick poke. Effective, yes... as the species does, indeed, perpetuate. Pleasurable? Hardly. Mere seconds of actual penetration. No "Was that good for you?" Scarcely anything worth lighting a cigarette after.

The fierceness of animal coitus and the pleasures of human copulation reside in 2 completely different realms. This observation can be added to your list of significant differences between animal consciousness and human consciousness... as you continue your ongoing compilation of What Makes Humans Human?

These sexness seminars are useful and informative. History and method. Skills. Style and technique. Vast and wide are the dimensions of human sexuality. As cultures and societies rise and fall... sexual customs and contrivances change and evolve over time. Doggy-style. Missionary position. She's on top. Use of lips and tongue for more than just kissing. *Kama Sutra.* This is a subject definitely worthy of being updated and informed about as you cruise into your upcoming incarnation. We, here at The Interpretorium, are dedicated to equipping you to enjoy pleasurable intimate experiences... both sensual and sexual... while you are Human on Planet Earth. Enjoyable, light-filled eroticism for all concerned.

❦ ❦ ❦

There are a lot of humans incarnate on Planet Earth. All at the same time. You will be amazed.

Right now... there are more than 7 billion peeps. More than 7 billion individual... thinking... feeling... sustaining units. That's... a lot. As you are there... busy being human... you will be so wrapped up in what is happening inside you and outside you... your plans... your opinions... your family... your career. Your choice of paint chips... your hair style... your chores. What's for dinner? Did anyone go to the market?

Your insights. Your judgments. Your triumphs. Your tragedies. It will hardly ever occur to you to consider those other 7 billion incarnate units... the vastness of their own perpetual experiencing. Each with their own triumphs... tragedies... beliefs... discernments. Seldom will you ponder this immense variety of livingness unfolding simultaneously in every moment.

Nearly every possible human thing that can happen on Planet Earth is happening in every present moment. The Perpetual Procedural Cacophony of Life. In every moment... a woman is giving birth... a first breath is drawn. A parent cuddles their child... a parent strikes their child. A person exhales their last breath. A loved one is shocked by their

The Ever-Exhilarating Bliss of Pure Light Consciousness

passing. Someone is getting dressed. A person sings. Someone wakes up. Someone sneezes. Someone is in pain. A person laughs... a group of people laugh together. Someone is meditating. Or medicating. Someone wins... someone loses. Conflict ensues. Grace occurs. All happening. All the time.

Each minute... 250 new souls get born on Planet Earth. Nurses and doctors... families and midwives... are there to welcome. To catch. Present at that first breath... those first cries. Witness... as the new one slides across that crucial incoming threshold. Life arrives.

On the day you arrive... 360,000 other new incarnate beings will also be transitioning in. All over the planet. Every day. Consider the welcoming parents... siblings... grandparents... family... community. This one arena alone... the new baby merry-go-round... diapers... nourishment... holding the sweet, new babe. Preparing, cooking, cleaning for the new family. Helping out. Taking pictures... sending pictures... sleep-deprivation... laundry... way too much gear... initiates for over 1,000,000 humans in each 24-hour period.

At the other end of Life: Within the human family... 110 people draw their last breath at the same minute in time. Disengaging. Their loved ones enmeshed in loss and sadness. Preparations have been made... or soon will be. Preparing the body... the memorial service... funeral... cremation... burial plot. Certified death documentation...

the will... the trust. The executrix... official documents... legal considerations. Each day... at least 152,000 people cross their Terminus Threshold back into pure, cognizant reality. Welcome home.

Human Life roars with perpetual activity. It is almost more than the human mind can comprehend. Busyness. So much... on... going... busy... ness. The continuous rush... the miraculous unfolding... of human activity. The cacophony of Life.

Living Life. The "All"... happening *all* the time. The "Individual"... ongoing consideration of myriad personal details. Each individual is the only one who gives "context" to the various "pieces" of their own kit. Each person gives meaning to their own Life and awareness. To their own accumulation of details and stuff.

The way those details fit together... the determinations... the bits... the pieces... the treasures... the jumble... is each person's individual concern. Dumping out the junk drawer. Each human determines why each of those bits and associated pieces are personally noteworthy. Life-shaping. Yet... as you are being human... rarely will you ever consider... "In the context of my Life... what makes this acquisition so significant?" "How is it this realization is so uplifting to me?" "Why does *this* trinket have the sentimental value I bestow upon it?" "Why is *this particular* occurrence of utmost importance?" Personal details.... your details... will rule your Life. Yet hardly ever will you consciously contemplate context.

This can be seen as the reason so many humans are overwhelmed by their gear. Their cargo. Their stuff. "I can hardly get this drawer closed. What *is* all this stuff?" "How can this closet... basement... garage... storage unit... be so crammed full?!" "I don't have time to deal with *all this stuff.*"

The art of human procrastination. Ahhhh... an art form of consequence. Procrastination is not the ally it pretends to be. This is an insight worth adding to your list of How to Manage Human Life on The Physical Plane. And it's a wily one. Procrastination says... "You don't have time to... read this... deal with this... sort thru this... right now. You can do it later." Note to self: "Later" never comes. When "later" does arrive... rarely is it "a better time" to... read... deal with... sort. When you get to "later"... it's already full of its own busyness. Its own things to read, sort, deal with. Thus do piles accumulate.

Why just crastinate... when you can go pro!?

Oh... here's another note of clarification... you may hear fellow humans say... "The devil is in the details." That's a misread. Truth be known... it's God who is in those details. Every "detail" is an opportunity to open to the current moment... to be present within the ongoing essence of Life. Or... to cram and slam and "just get this over with!"

In our most recent Orientation Moment... we delved into how it all be happening as you cross the threshold into your new incarnation and get born into your upcoming human Life. In this session we will touch upon the other end... your Terminus Threshold. The timing and organic processes as you exit incarnation. As you pass back into the vast reality of sublime cognitive energy. Into Light.

In incarnation... as you are "individualized"... you establish the architecture of your own frames of reference. Your own context. The set of Life criteria that is yours. Constructed upon the scaffolding of your beliefs and inner response mechanisms. Colored by the consequences of outer determinants and influences.

Your context... your Life environment... can be steeped in knick-knacks, mementos, and nostalgia. Or... crisp and orderly... no extra frills. You get to choose.

The setting... the circumstances... each attitude and contrivance... gives meaning to the events, connexions, and components of a Life. *Your* meaning. Occurrences and realizations are... or can be... brought into full understanding. Your understanding. Your context.

Many people allow their fear to guide their choices and create their context. This usually leads to fright... self-inflicted limitation... constriction. "Us" vs "them." Anxiety, dread and foreboding rule their Life... inner and outer. Paralyzing their growth. Making their world a fearsome place. It is, after all, their creation.

As you are embraced by your transition back into Light... the context of your Life... choices you have made... who you have become... the realizations you bring back with you... are assessed. This evaluation process breeds and generates your ongoing awareness capabilities in future incarnations.

In the midst of accumulating, juggling and dealing with all of your Life details and requirements... as you grow into your human adulthood... a moment comes. Comprehension dawns. This is all so finite. My Life is going to be over at some point. Possibly sooner than later. I do not have an inexhaustible supply of time to knock around here being human. I could have 3 more days or 37 years. A penetrating realization.

The great unknown is so totally... unknown.

As you inhabit your incarnate instrument, you... and your thoughts, words and deeds... are beholden to your shelf life. Obligated to reside between your first breath and your last. No more. No less.

Human energy units on other planets live longer than Earthtone humans. This is attributed to each individual's instrumentation being more inclined to comply with guidance... to obey awareness... as they strive to create a Life in accordance with the common good. This stance leads to less wear and tear on the tri-body unit... mental, emotional and physical.

On both Euripdiacez and Kanohaloa, their humanosity span is closer to 500 years. Of course, this enables much karmic and dharmic handiwork to be accomplished. On these 2 planets, it is rare for breath allotments to be less than 100 years. All children grow to adulthood.

You can check out the Euripdiacez and Kanohaloa Playbooks for longevity tips and healthful reminders.

Planet Earth humans call their span of incarnate years "Life expectancy." How long can we expect a Life to be? I expect there is an assortment of factors involved:

1. Inherited genetic material... physical and psycho logical
2. Behaviors, habits and general usage of time
3. Environmental pollutants and conditions
4. The degree of mindful nurturance... individually and collectively

One must also take into consideration Planet Earth's speedy spin as it revolves around its sun. Whoosh! A real fly by! Taking only 365 "days" for a complete orbit makes for a quick and rugged ride. Then you add in the factor of Planet Earth's own rapid rotation... whipping around on its axis every 24 "hours." Other human-inhabited planets do their orbiting differently. Not quite so much spin and whirl. Slower planetary sequencing proves to be gentler on the terrestrial human apparatus. Kinder to the aquatic rhythms and Life forms as well.

Earth: Spinning. Revolving. Rapidly rotating. Oh my!

Of course, also included in this mix is the compelling force of gravity. On the surface of Planet Earth… gravity does a splendid job keeping the whole shebang in place. But it does rub and fray. Much swirleriffic activity + the constant tug of gravity = Whew! All this gyrating tension wears soundly on the fragile human instrument.

This assortment of divergent dynamics does factor into shelf life expiration. AKA… death. Not many humans incarnate on Earth manage to surpass their century mark. When they do… especially impressive are those centenarians who manage to retain their "spry and sharp" capabilities.

Knowing how little time you actually have on Planet Earth adds to the poignancy… the sweetness… of Life. For many incarnate humans… the sweetness of Life turns bitter as thoughts of death intensify their terror.

Currently… especially in "the Western World"… cultural convention sees death as a negative. Something to be avoided. Ha! Like *that's* going to happen. Death does, after all, reside in the realm of that which cannot be disputed.

Ignorance about the transition of death abounds. This fright and denial = less than empowering.

In the human view... colored by the grief and pain experienced by those "left behind"... death is presumed to be a hardship on the dying. Compared to the psychological suffering of those being consumed by sorrow and loss... the one who "goes away"... the one who dies... generally has the easier part to play.

The actual arrival of your death may be quick or slow. Completely unexpected... or long and drawn out. It may be you get absolutely no time to "think about it." Or... you could get lots of time... to consider... contemplate... deny... tussle. Perhaps even time to come to a place of peaceful resignation. Surrender. Acceptance.

This is true also for those who care about you. Your quick passing hits as a harsh, unexpected blow. It can knock the wind right out of the ones who love you. Or... when drawn out... your loved ones are given time to adjust to your upcoming departure. Altho... even when the process is long and drawn out... once the moment of death actually arrives... it is always a shock. Too final.

For humans... rather than bringing a deep and certain peace... awareness of death frequently instigates panic. As humans realize how little time they actually have... they freak. Resulting in a paralyzing dread of the unpredictable.

People make up all kinds of stories about where they go after death. "Heaven?" "Hell?" "Eaten by maggots?" "Who knows where?!" They torment themselves thinking about loved ones they will lose to death. Aware that death can, literally, happen at any moment solidifies their mortal fright. This panic of projection ... this self-terrorizing... presides over much heartache. And many a poor decision.

The span of your Planet Earth incarnation... threshold to threshold... how many days, months, or years you are assigned to live in your human package... is determined by the number of breaths commissioned in your Breath Allotment Packet. This number is firm. As mentioned... no more... no less. When you are in human form... there is no way to add breaths to... nor subtract breaths from... your current incarnant allotment.

Breaths. An inhale + its accompanying exhale = 1 breath. A yawn... 1 big inhale + 1 big exhale = 1 breath. A gasp... 1 quick intake of breath + 1 exhale = 1 breath. A sigh... 1 inhale + 1 exhale (with or without vocalization) = 1 breath.

As we consider human physiology... a healthy adult, at rest, draws about 16 breaths per minute. This calculates to a little fewer than 1,000 breaths per hour... 23,200 breaths per day. The average human draws over 8,000,000 breaths in the span of a year. Your Breath Allotment Packet can contain anywhere from 1 breath to *777,777,777* breaths per lifetime. Occasionally, more than 777,777,777 breaths are allotted. This may sound like a swell idea… more time on Planet Earth. But, I gotta tell ya… by the time you've gotten to nearly 800 million breaths… your Bio Energy Navigation Gear is pretty well spent. Nearly *kaput*. Your shelf-life is wavering. You're about to drop off-line.

Breath generates your activity quotient. "I'm here!"

What makes your human Life groovy or gross? This is completely determined by what you choose to do with your time… your thoughts… your attitudes… your creativity… your actions… between your first breath and your last.

Singing… dancing. Cursing… bullying. Fighting. Forgiving.

Your breath allotment embeds within Your Etheric Sconce. Your total number of breaths is an item of incarnant information which is completely veiled from your conscious human awareness. There are incarnants who have dreams or insights about their death… seeing the way they will die. But thinking in terms of the number of breaths you have been allotted… not likely that will ever cross your mind.

In some planetary realms… a warning system is in place… "Advisement: You are approaching your last 750,000 breaths." So helpful for getting affairs in order. This was tried for a short while on Planet Earth. Eons ago. It was not a good fit for humanness. For an Earthtone human…

knowledge of final days... well... it created more panic than orderly affairs.

"Wait! I'm not done yet!" = the frequent human lament. You may have noticed... nowhere in your sheaf of incarnant agreements will you find any guarantee stating you will have finished all of your projects and undertakings before you depart. Nor will you stay in incarnation until you get all your drawers or closets cleaned out and organized. Every "i" will not be dotted. Every "t" will not get crossed. The vast number of times... as a human draws their last breath... there are myriad things left unsaid... undone. And a lot of "stuff" to sort thru.

Still, this smattering of foreknowledge... you may breathe your last at any moment... can be used as a good reason to take stock... evaluate... sort and toss. Set yourself some priorities. Make the best version of the Life you've got left.

Thru-out the centuries... a limited number of humans have had "near death" experiences. Prompted by a variety of different causes... their Life Force ebbs... and they seem to place a step upon their Terminus Threshold. They are given a glimpse of the magnificence offered by crossing this Threshold. Then they are called back to resume their incarnant Life. Frequently... near always... the immense, mind-blowing reality of their brief Threshold experience has a profound impact. Genuinely effecting the way they live the rest of their resumed incarnation.

These "near death" experiences may appear haphazard. They're not. Due to humankind's ungainly fear of death... their profound self-terrorizing factor... these "near death" experiences have been deemed advisable to give humans some hints... a few clues... as to what they may find waiting "on the other side." Those who "return" to Life... recounting what they saw and felt... bear witness to the super-physical mysteries... the alchemy of Life. We offer these "near death" episodes to put to rest some of the unfounded human fear around death.

In many cases, the transition experience does indeed include a "tunnel of Light." And, yes, there may be loved ones waiting to greet the incoming. Energetically... it plays out a little differently than that. But humans do find great comfort in the thought of being greeted. The truth is... you *are* warmly greeted. By Love. Frequently, that Love makes a "visual representation" in the form of previously departed loved ones welcoming you home.

Some humans may find it comforting to know that "on the other side" there are "viewing platforms"... for the recently departed to observe loved ones they have just left. For the departed... the emotional tug is no longer part of the equation. But they do get to "watch" whenever they'd like. For as long as they'd like. As you have seen for yourself here in cognizant reality... these "viewing" options can be called upon... to observe the activities of daily living... the highlights and the lowlights... of those who still reside in human form. This is an accommodation. A being of pure cognant energy can "go for a view" any time they are inclined.

The intertwining connexion between breath and death elucidates The Great Mystery of Life. And The Great Neuroses. There are humans who occasionally ponder this Mystery. Some find it quite intriguing. For the many others... it never crosses their minds. Just as well.

When your "time comes"... a human euphemism... you may experience mild nausea... a few odd, numb-tingly sensations... perhaps a moment or 2 of puzzlement. Then you pass into Light.

Each human approaches their Terminus Threshold differently. As mentioned... some have known it was coming and were able to "prepare" a bit. Others don't even realize they've left incarnation until they find themselves in The Afterglow. "Whoa! It's over already!? How'd *that* happen?"

The instant you re-merge into Total Awareness... Life streams on. Without skipping a beat. You soar along in the ever-exhilarating Bliss of Pure Light Consciousness. All. Is. Oh. So. Swell.

As I mentioned... Life's poignancy is colored by how little time you actually get to be on Planet Earth.

Ah yes, speaking of priorities to engage while incarnate... here's a good one... tell the people you love that you love them. Show the people you love that you love them. Let them know how much you value them... and how important they are to you and your well-being. Especially the younglings in your Life.

The "pain of death" is felt only by those who remain in the human world. Friends and family who remain incarnate can find it quite wrenching as a loved one exits incarnation. Dealing with the trauma of your death... those you "left behind" should not have to wonder if they were loved by you.

For humans... death holds an ancient terror. The tragedy, of course, is that most people only see or relate to the incarnant body. There can be resuscitation efforts... keeping a spent body "alive" with tubes and machines... forcing oxygen and Life-sustaining fluids. In desperation... some may attempt to reinstate the body by giving it what it once wanted or needed... pure water... healthy food... tender words... whispering the Secrets of the Universe in their ear. To no avail. It is now perfectly clear... in no uncertain terms. Once the animating force has left the body... once consciousness is withdrawn... all attempts to resuscitate are for naught. The one who has died is, indeed, free. Liberated from bondage. Swallowed up in victory.

As you cross your Terminus Threshold... any physical or psychological pain you may have been feeling is alleviated the instant you transition. It's all just gone. Your cloak of hurt and botheration simply evaporates. Those human doubts and insecurities are no longer necessary... no longer viable. You clearly see... and feel... what a construct... what a fabrication... your human Life has been. The woes... the wailing... the lamentations... based only on short sight.

For centuries... there have been humans who recognize death as The Law of Liberation. An accurate assessment. For that is what death offers. That is what death does. Death liberates.

Oh, I do want to mention... when you are incarnate... even as liberation from human difficulty and despair might sound like the relief you are looking for... it is never worthwhile to end your own Life. The very act itself sets up a series of karmic repercussions... physical and psychological.

Altho there are always a vast number of options... in The Great Scheme of Things, suicide is never a good idea. Especially do not poison your body. And don't shoot yourself in the head. It takes eons for the etheric web supporting your future incarnant bodies to recover. To adjust. To move on. To again be viable Incarnate Navigation Gear.

To an anguished mind, death may seem "the answer." A smooth way out of desperation or depression. It is not the sleek escape you might be looking for. Self-inflicted death reverberates thru-out Your Etheric Sconce... setting in place a calcifying texture which takes many future incarnations... and karmic endeavors... to reconfigure. Simply put... suicide is not the easy solution a desperate incarnate human is hoping to find.

As you cross the Terminus Threshold at the end of your incarnation... your experience of being freed from the mortal body begins with a *whoosh*... an immediate lift in consciousness. You will be human... in your physical body one moment... and the very next... drawn back into Light. And just as actively conscious there. Uh, here.

Life... death... one continuous activity. Consciousness... awareness... one continuous stream. There is no death... only different states of being. The "other side" of death is simply being. Being in another dimension. The door to that dimension is within your individual energy field. At a certain point in time, you step thru that door. Out of one suit of clothing... into another. Physical death is scarcely more than a change in form. A different venue. The scenery altered.

Here is where it gets tricky for the human mind to comprehend. The Great Beyond is not "up" or "out." It is *in*.

The Ever-Exhilarating Bliss of Pure Light Consciousness

When you are human... the limiting fixation of perceiving in only 3 dimensions makes this concept of "in" challenging to grasp.

Using as an example the vocabulary of the Christian explaining tradition... the Avatar Jesus is quoted as saying, "The Kingdom of Heaven is within you." Here... the use of the word "Heaven"... including reference to Heaven's "many mansions"... endeavors to explain the many interpenetrating levels and realms. The many strata of Life and consciousness... which are, indeed, within each and every human.

Humans have interpreted "Heaven" as a place "above us"... "in the sky." One does not literally "ascend" to heaven... there is no physical heaven anywhere in the universe. In the course of this past century... human knowledge gained thru physics and astronomy has eliminated any thought of "heaven" as a literal, physical possibility. It could be said... even if ascending at the speed of light ... Jesus... or anyone else... would still be in the galaxy.

Let us investigate the passage "Jesus ascended to heaven" as the metaphor it is intended to be. Clearly, Jesus enters... not into outer space... but into *inward* space. Into the Spark of Life Within. The place from which all being comes. A cosmic longitude and latitude... deep in inner consciousness. An energy vortex... into and thru which we pass. The Life consciousness that is The Source of all things.

This is the same energy that slows its gradient pace as you enter incarnation. Slowing to accommodate... and "match"... the lucid interface within your mental, emotional, and physical human Life. As you pass out of incarnation... you pass into and thru this very Spark of Life which animates your human instrument. The Seed of All Being Awareness. The Kingdom of Heaven Within.

A world closer than breath itself.

Being here, you well know... crossing the Terminus Threshold... returning home... you are immediately surrounded by... infused with... wondrous, profound Light. Sweet Relief. Soothing. Elevating. Enlightening. Euphoric. Joy-radiating. Drinking in the Love of God's Smile. Rapture.

Here in cognizant reality, you know exactly what I'm talking about. Human language, however, is sorely limited in its ability to convey the marvel... the spaciousness... the grace... of this Light-filled realm.

I know this all makes great sense to you... as you sit here, now. But... oh, that humanosity. Talk about tying your shoelaces together at the beginning of the race. Beyond language and vocabulary... beyond concepts and resistance... lies that riveting human belief in being separate from God. Separate from... and in most cases, unaware of... the All Love Life Force. That B.I.A.S.... that false Belief I Am

Separate... generates and fuels the human fear of death. If humans believed and knew... I Am One With God. One with The Force of Life. There would be no terror around death. Calm composure would prevail. The grace of the transition... the grace of liberation... would be clear. Welcomed.

You would indeed go in peace.

At this point... I will take a moment to acknowledge the number of you in this Orientation Pod who have signed on for The Privilege of Growing Older. Your interest in remaining in your incarnant form into your later years has been duly noted. This intent to age in place... to wear the same human kit for many decades... can be very useful. Allowing you a good possibility to fulfill your incarnating purpose... and work thru greater intervals of karmic activity.

An observation worth sharing... youth can be seen as a gift of nature. Age is a work of art.

As your B.E.I.N.G. remains stable and fit for use... all is swell. However, you'll recall we have previously mentioned... as your human years accumulate and you move into your 60s, 70s, and 80s... physical bio-processes begin to slow down and "the body aging" comes upon you. Currently, your Bio Navigation Gear is configured to last for a century or less. After "middle age"... continuing to accumulate years as you spin around the sun... your bio-energy decreases. The physical body can begin to develop... weakness... limitations... processing glitches. This decline is not a requirement. Altho it does happen in most cases. Your genetics and diverse inherited characteristics... as well as Life choices and healthy habits... play a significant role in the way the aging process infiltrates your human instrument.

Along with declining physical energy... your mental and emotional procedural activities may begin to display the effects of your accumulating years. These would be the aforementioned "processing problems." For some aging humans, a plaque develops in the brain which slows mental function... affecting memory synapses... distorting cognitive reality... altering one's personality. The act of recalling information... recollecting Life's pertinent details... becomes sketchy. Initially... you might find it helpful to make lists... to write things down. Notes to self. Even more than usual. Then comes the tricky part... remembering where you put those notes and lists.

For many, human old age is an enigmatic source of irony... paradox... incongruity. Questions unanswered. Goals not met. Closets not straightened. Where did the time go?

There are many coping mechanisms... some truly worthwhile... others, not that effective. Wry amusement = a worthwhile approach. Both for the declining elder and for those offering care. Perspective is the ally it promises to be.

The Ever-Exhilarating Bliss of Pure Light Consciousness

I am inspired to remind you... as you draw your first incarnant breath... your Life is instantly on "play." Your human instrument is equipt with neither a "pause" nor a "rewind" function. You are awash in the ongoing. The rushing current of being alive. No dress rehearsals. Precious few 2nd chances. You're taking it all in "on the fly." (Gotta love those human aphorisms.) You make do with the best you are able to offer in any given moment. You dance... you gyrate... you reel... to the music. The Great Symphony of Life. Many obstacle illusions. Many obscure delusions. Many kind moments of grace. They all play out. Looking so real. Feeling so real. Playing so real.

Death arrives in a heartbeat. Your last allotted breath. A period (.) at the end of your sentence. Beyond dispute.

The extraction process occurs. The seed of Inner/Higher Light Consciousness that animates your B.E.I.N.G. is freed. Returning to Light.

Here you are! Back in Bliss.

As you re-engage this realm of elation... this loving continuation of Life... you maintain the awareness... the understanding and knowledge you gained during your visit to earth. There will be opportunities to debrief... to re-view your incarnate occurrences and all that transpired. Your errors and foibles. Your successes and accomplishments. Your kindnesses and compassion.

All is acknowledged. All is released. All is forgiven. Transformed.

Jewels of realization accumulate in your etheric vault. Light penetrates your entirety. There is no room for blame... sin... guilt... shame. These are revealed to be the constricting human constructs they are. Human reaction to human behavior. Those rules and patterns no longer apply. Sweet release.

Zippy Zingo!! Oh, What A Ride!

We are now going to take a short break. Intermission. Recess. Earlier, you were each issued a "watch"... an instrument to watch time. These are handy devices for being aware of the "movement of time" in the human sense. These watches we've distributed are designed to either be worn on your wrist or kept in a pocket in your clothing. The watch you have received is of the "analog" variety. It has a "face" and "hands," which humans have used to "keep track of time" for centuries. Incarnating into modern day environs... you will find there are now also "digital" timepieces. They perform the same time-tracking function... the information simply displays differently. Familiarize yourself with this analog way time is "kept." Using your watch... watching the "hands" on the "face"... bring yourself back here in 30 minutes. Which is also known as "half an hour."

The food court is open. At this time... we prefer you not bring food or beverages back with you. Crumbs... spills... you know.

When you come back and get settled... we will again enjoy the insights and good humor of our Recent Returnee. Have a nice break.

※ ※ ※

Aloha nearly incarnant humans. I am glad to be back here with you all. Interestingly... I was about to ask if I could return to speak with you. Then I was invited to return to speak with you. Properly serendipitous, that.

Right off the bat... which is a human colloquialism... meaning "at the very beginning"... I want to say again... if you have any questions... inquiries... any wonderings... anything "on your mind" before you enter your upcoming incarnation... please feel welcome to turn your thoughts in my direction. Think of me... and I will be in touch. Hopefully, I will be able to respond to your query in a helpful manner.

When invited to return here to speak with you... I was specifically asked to convey some of my recent human awareness notes in the realm of forgiveness. I heard mentioned before your break... when you arrive back in Light... "all is forgiven."

Keep in mind... transgressions are processed differently here in cognent reality than they are on Earth. Undoubtedly, you recall from previous post-incarnant debriefs... the systems of checks and balances are applied in a different manner here than in the human realm. The dharmic carousel... the karmic resource council... interpret "all is forgiven" as you letting go of your particular poo. As you embracing, interpreting and assimilating insights and awarenesses your human poo presented you... in all its glory and obfuscation.

Karmically speaking... your "all" continues to be an issue and offer insight. "All" that has happened in your current human Life is delved into... queried... adjusted... modified. Then remodeled and repurposed. Fabricated into evolving karmic Life patterns for future discernment and motifs of living. Conduct appearing to be against The One... against compassion, insight and clear vision... leads to calibrated reprisals. Your Etheric Sconce is prepped and eventually recirculated back into the incarnating system. Where it will be primed for future "learning opportunities." Lessons. Based on the concoction of your past realizations and actions. These future Life lessons you have, in fact, created for yourself. Shaped thru your own incarnant choices and activities. You'll hear in the human realm... "What goes around comes around." Indeed.

Navigating the human realm... you will definitely discover this for yourself... but seeing as we're here, I am just going to tell you... the majority of incarnate humans are all kinds of fascinated with hanging on to their poo. Their gripes and grudgement. This is a remarkable human conundrum. Clinging to resentment... revisiting slights... festering bitterness. Humans seem to hold it dear. "*My* painful poo." *My* bitterness. Fostering a culture of grievance. Holding on to hurt and ill will. Rather than... oh, I don't know... just *letting go* of the turmoil and agitation.

(I mean, *really*... where does holding onto it ever get you?)

Many humans are ruled by their inner agitation and the babble of their negative psycho logical content. "No way am I just letting go of my hatred and hostility! I work hard to be this angry!" "I've got to avenge and punish!" Ooooh... be careful with that one. Good way to bite yourself... hard.

The truth is... you have just so much time... just so much precious, personal, incarnate energy. Hanging onto resentment and slights... hanging onto your tantrums... offers such a narrow, limited outlook.

The take-away? Narrow, limited Life results.

Bitterness, animosity and ill will grind a hostile lens thru which to view your human world. Delivering distorted Life content. Believe me... plenty more productive, fun and worthwhile ways of being are available to you as you experience your fleeting... yet momentous... human Life.

What you see... what you tell yourself... is what you get. "My Life sucks. How can I inflict harm?" "My Life is a blessing. How can I help?" I know... you have heard this before. The truth of it = so pervasive. It is well worth mentioning again.

You will find many humans seem to think hanging onto resentment and bitterness... "not forgiving"... causes the "other person" to suffer. Seriously? Ix-nay on at-thay. You want to say to these folks... consider this... that "other person" probably doesn't even *remember* you. It's highly unlikely they even recall the painful incident you are hanging onto. And hurting yourself with time and again. Each time you focus on this emotional roadkill, you are stung anew.

You are hurting yourself.

Here at The Interpretorium... sitting in cognent reality... you are well aware:

Forgiveness is of far greater advantage to the forgiver than it is to the forgiven.

The forgiver wins.

Humans have a hard time seeing it this way. The human psyche gets fritzed... mired... stuck... thinking that making it a point to personally hang onto pain and resentment... rehashing self-inflicted humiliation... will somehow cause more punishment to the person who inflicted the perceived harm. It doesn't.

Rehashing inner resentment is like scratching off an emotional scab, time and again. This not only thwarts the healing process... in fact, you open yourself to psycho logical inflammation and serious emoto infection. You are punishing yourself. Some humans see this clearly. Others continue to penalize themselves as they twist in the spin cycle... the delusion of retribution and "payback."

Take a moment to engage your Recall + Retain Button as you contemplate *this* bit of revealing insight: Not forgiving someone is like drinking poison and expecting the other person to die. Likelihood of that happening? Zip. Hanging onto and regurgitating hostility and bitterness only poisons *your* Life. Your ongoing upset and recurring vitriol gets *you* a'churnin' and a'burnin'. It has very little effect on the "other person."

It's easy to see... bemoaning the discomfort of acid-reflux has no effect on the food that caused it. No uncomfortable belch ever made a chili dog say, "Oh, sorry about that." Yet humans, feeling wronged... seem to believe their emotional acid-reflux: "I'll show them! I will *never* forgive!" Like this is going to result in the perceived perpetrator feeling remorseful or punished. Likely not.

Biologically... "I'll never forgive" proves to be untrue. The human brain is graced with the gift of neuroplasticity = the brain's astounding super power to reorganize, change and adapt. Grace, indeed. This adaptation attribute is much valued by beings who are looking to incarnate. As you know, this is a primary reason Planet Earth is noted as A Prime Human Incarnate Experience.

Neuroplasticity easily offers human beings all the agility and resilience required for forgiveness.

The pliant flexibility of the human brain and nervous system is prized. That unique neuron activity... and its nimble restructuring... allows you the ongoing formation of new neural connections from your birth to the very end of Life. The human brain has the capacity to reorganize synaptic links... reshaping neural conductivity. This allows the brain and nervous system to adjust in response to new or changing conditions, situations and input. To respond rather than merely react. To transform rather than calcify.

As it turns out... the capacity for forgiveness is an intrinsic part of human nature. Inborn. Part of the equipment. Both software and hardware are called into play. Your choice.

Forgiveness is a capacity available to exercise. An ability in which to excel.

The Ever-Exhilarating Bliss of Pure Light Consciousness

The hardware = the brain's functional biology… its synaptic links and neural conductivity. The software = your ability to psycho logically choose.

Are you "weak" if you don't "strike back?" Weak if you don't "hold on" to grievance? If you don't tussle? "I'll show them!" Really? Who would that be, actually? Who are you going to "show?" Exactly what are you going to "show them?"

Observing this ongoing human pickle… you sometimes just want to shout… "Are you kidding me?!" "Come on you humans! Let's grow!"

You can do this. Exercise your capacity to forgive. Don't short-change yourself.

When you are established in your human instrument, you will find forgiveness is a practice. A self-training. Like exercising your gratitude muscle. Or choosing to respond rather than react. *Choose* to stop feeling tweaked. *Choose* to stop holding on to anger and grievance. Just let it go. Choose to release yourself from self-harm and grumble. Choose some more. Practice.

Coach yourself to let go of blaming others.

Coach yourself to let go of blaming yourself.

As you are human… remind yourself to let go of self-calcifying vengeance. Practice: "I will no longer let my resentment over past taunts and offenses rule my Life."

Because this *is* what happens. Your resentment rules your Life. Bitterness overtakes your inner world. Pollutes your inner environment.

You are hurting yourself. Victimized by your own attachment to feeling offended. Blinded by the unthinking clamor of grievance... and the need to "do something about it."

Your urge to retaliate... to regurgitate... hardens the way you view your world. Bitterness begets bitterness. Holding your bitterness and resentment close... in a tight grip... causes you to make ill-considered decisions and choices. You're being pushed around... oppressed... by your own destructive hostility.

Fixating on revenge is a waste of your precious time.

In the long ago in human history on Earth... Confucius, a revered sage from the land called China, wisely observed... "Before you embark on a journey of revenge... dig 2 graves."

Grievance is not the ally it pretends to be.

Vengeance solves nothing. It only grows itself... feeding the ongoing cycle of retaliation. "Tit" for "tat" just keeps on "titting" and "tatting." This need to "settle the score" only furthers distress... inflicting more torment and agony. Again. Absolutely nothing is "settled." You are being pranked.

While incarnate, you serve yourself well to remember… forgiveness is a conscious decision. A deliberate act. Forgiveness is your choice. These insights are well-worth engaging your Recall + Retain Function to instill them in your human awareness. Your incarnant instrument comes equipt with an inborn capacity to release yourself from feelings of resentment or vengeance toward those you feel have wronged you.

Holding on to grudgement only sours *you*. Whether you feel the other person "deserves" your forgiveness. Or not. Release yourself from your ruinous malcontent.

Forgiveness does not change the past.

Forgiveness changes the future.

Somebody has got to break the repeating cycle of vengeance and retaliation. It's gonna happen sometime. Grievance lacks imagination. It doesn't always get to win. Somebody's got to shut it on antagonistic taunts and spectacles. There are alternatives. You have options. Different… more constructive… ways to deal. Somebody has to make more creative, conciliatory choices. Somebody has to be willing to heal. To move on. It may as well be you.

Forgiving… letting go… is for *you*. Not "them."

The question of whether "they" deserve your forgiveness is moot. Irrelevant. *You* deserve your forgiveness. You deserve to release yourself from feeling gutted… knotted up…

shamed. You deserve to free yourself from that emotional sewer. Fouled. Imprisoned by your own bitterness.

> Don't let "them" have that power over you.
> Don't give them the ongoing power
> to sour your inner Life.

> Release yourself
> from the corrosive need
> to hold on to resentment and anger.
> You *deserve* to forgive yourself.

Forgiveness is for your own peace of mind. Your own peace of being.

Forgive yourself for (what you may perceive as) your own "stupidity"… your own "naïveté." Your own lack of situational awareness. Your own poor choices.

Let yourself off the hook.

Release attachment. "I release my attachment to feeling bitter and distressed." You free yourself from corrosive anger. You free yourself to take your next steps forward. You proceed in your Life. No longer reminding yourself you have been wronged or taken advantage of. No longer weighed down by regurgitating hurtful feelings.

I see some of you looking a little startled… on Earth they would say, you look like "a deer in the headlights."

Baffled. Befuddled. "Why in the world would I hold onto corrosive resentment?!" "What *is* all this 'tangled up in bitterness'?" "Huh?"

I *know*. This psycho logical self-torture makes no sense. And yet… it will seem very real to your human self. This fixation on discord… on pain and slights and "not forgiving"… will impact your sensibilities and discolor your perceptions while you are a human of Earth.

In the ways of human interaction… as we speak of what forgiveness is… it is also of value to be clear about what forgiveness is *not*. As you forgive… you are neither denying nor glossing over your distress. Forgiveness does not mean you must forget… or condone… or excuse… the offense against you.

I want to be very clear here. Festering in your distress… you are the one who is punished by your own fritz and fright. Punished by your own anger and bitterness.

As you live your human Life… pain is inevitable. Suffering is optional.

There is no rule saying you must cling to pain and misery. No requirement that you must fester. Or suffer.

There is also no rule saying you are obligated to reconcile with the person you feel has harmed you. You are not required to feel all sunshine and sweetsie toward your offender. They *can* be banished from your Life. But… for yourself... choose to let go of deeply held hurt and anguish. Do not let doom and gloom own you. Do not let those anguished feelings win.

Forgive. Let go. Further your inner healing. Release. Move on with your Life. This choice... your practice of forgiveness... allows you to acknowledge the pain you suffered. Without letting that pain continue to define or deform you.

During my most recent incarnation... a senseless tragedy occurred which offered deep insight into the human capacity to forgive. Without provocation, a man... a father, a husband, a son... opened fire on a group of young girls in an Amish schoolhouse, killing 5 and wounding 5 others. These girls were ages 6 thru 13. He then killed himself.

The Amish are a sect of people who are known in their outer Life for simple living... plain dress... a reluctance to adopt many conveniences of modern technology. In their inner Life... "letting go of grudges" is rooted deep in their culture. You, yourself, may have been Amish in a former Life.

From the Amish perspective... extending forgiveness... a willingness to forgo vengeance... is not to undo the tragedy nor pardon the wrong. Rather... the Amish embrace forgiveness as a cleansing first step toward a more hopeful future.

Later in the same day this shooting occurred, an Amish grandfather was heard to say, "I don't think there's anybody here that wants to do anything but forgive." Not only did the Amish community reach out to their own who lost daughters at the schoolhouse... they also reached out to the family of the man who shot their innocent girls. Their stance of forgiveness and reconciliation was widely covered in the national media... deeply affecting people who heard the story. It certainly affected me.

Most humans who come to forgiveness... get there after going thru a long, psycho logical process. Amish people practice "decisional forgiveness." They forgive first. They make that decision. Then, each day, they work thru their emotions. Over a decade later... the Amish families were still consciously deciding... choosing... to forgive. Every day.

The youngest of the girls... 6-year-old Rosanna... was shot in the head. She did not die. She lives with severe brain damage... wheelchair-bound... neither speaking nor walking. Guided by their stance of reconciliation... the Amish community embraced the shooter's mother. Not long after the tragedy took place... at her request... she became part of the young girl's care team. One evening each week, the shooter's mother arrives at Rosanna's home to spend several hours taking care of her.

As Rosanna's father tends to his daughter's needs... he is reminded every day of the shooter and what he did. This does not change the goodwill he feels toward the shooter's mother. You can well imagine... this father's forgiveness does not come easily. Some Amish parents mourned the deaths of their daughters. For others... their wounded daughters have fully healed. Yes... Rosanna did survive. And her family also lost her. She will never be herself again.

Every day, her father fights back his anger. Every day, he has to forgive anew. Rosanna's father remarks, "I've always said, and continue to say, we have a lot of hard work to be what the people brag about us to be."

As I stand before you here today... not for 1 minute am I saying forgiveness is easy in the human Life mechanism. For some... it may be. Perhaps they make the choice to let it be easy. For most humans forgiveness can be hard work. Exercise. Diligence. Practice.

When you are human... you must be strong... resolved. "I will not be consumed by bitterness." You must not allow grudgement, resentment and vengeance to twist your Life... inner or outer.

Do not let bitterness win.

In the larger scheme of things... as an incarnate human... your ability to forgive is a significant game-changer. In ways you will not even comprehend while you are in human form. As you forgive... you release yourself... from the entanglements of current incarnate attachments. You are no longer compelled to cling to strictures of unnecessary burden. Your gift to yourself of forgiving... releasing...

unburdening… allows you to reconcile and harmonize inner strife with long-standing karmic empath factors.

While this is unlikely to even cross your mind as you are being human…. be advised… resolving karmic entanglements while you're in human form is the key opportunity to release and reconcile. Which means you don't carry these useless emotional snares back here with you… to then be incorporated into your future Etheric Sconce "issues" and tensions. Save your future incarnant instrument wear and tear. Actualize this truth:

> Forgiveness releases you.
> Forgiveness empowers you.

Speaking of empowerment and karmic factors… thinking of returning to you here in The Interpretorium… I had some specific matters I wanted to talk with you about. Since I my last visit with you… I have been occupied with my incarnant debrief… officially known as the I.E.I. The Incarnant Exit Interview. (They kept it simple.) As you complete your mission: Human on Planet Earth, you debrief. Your incarnant choices and realizations are examined and evaluated. They are then catalogued, archived and eventually woven into the fabric of your future karmic energy sheath. These debriefing interviews and discussions are always revealing and insightful.

They are also a great opportunity for in-depth conversations with other Recent Returnees. As we were in debrief... I mentioned I had been here with you and we had spoken of the relationships between human parents and their children. Well, *that* opened a floodgate. Leading to intriguing conversations as other Returnees processed recollections based on their recent human youngling experiences.

Many of these Returnees... as human children... experienced cellular recollection of growing up in other Planetary Realms. Realms where children are treated with much more attentive caring and respect than they are on Planet Earth. In most cases, these recollections did not appear as actual clear memories. Rather, these etheric recollections had enough impact on the psyche to make the child... and the adult they became... feel something was just "not right" with the way they were treated as younglings of Earth.

I realized in the midst of these post-debrief conversations... in the interest of informing you as effectively as possible... I wanted to return to your Orientation Pod and share with you a few more useful bits of parent/child elucidation and technique. Style points.

As I mentioned... I was here before you left on your break. I heard your Tour Guide's suggestions to "Tell the people you love that you love them." I totally concur. There's even a popular song in the 20th century... "Shower the people you love with love... show them the way you feel. Things are gonna be much better if you only will." True dat.

I completely agree with the guidance you received to let the people you love... especially your children... know you *value* them. Let them know they are important to you. Let them know they touch your heart.

I will also add... as your children grow older... let them know you approve of the way they are living their Life. Don't quibble. Let your adult children know you respect their choices. Even when you question their decisions. Even when you know you are "right."

Disapproval is not the Life ally it pretends to be.

You would not believe how many people crave hearing approval from their parents. Even a small acknowledging kindness. Or "Good job!" from their bosses and colleagues. You will find... humans are a bit lax in expressing positive acknowledgment. Are they afraid of affirming others? Maybe it simply does not occur to most humans to mention the favorable and encouraging.

It seems humans have no limit to finding fault. In this current Earthtone time frame, with the anonymity of "social media"... criticism and hostility are tossed around frequently. Compliments and approval... not so much.

You will be struck by what an issue this is for humans... feeling valued. More than likely, you will experience the absence of it yourself.

Based on my earlier visit with this Orientation Pod, I know it is important to many of you to become a good human parent. The conversations I had with other Planet Earth Returnees inspired me to return here with 3 significant parenting elements to bring to your attention.

I am going to share with you something I have experienced in many of my own human childhoods. Most of the Recent Returnees I've spoken with tell me this was an issue for them, as well.

Neglect... benign and otherwise. The majority of human parents treat their children as if there is always something more important to do than be present with the kids. Especially in "developed" countries... as parents are with their children... they frequently have their nose in their personal electronic devices... the television or a video game... a book or newspaper. Many times, the parent is impatient and snappish. As if the kids are a nuisance... a bother. Adults always seem to have something "more important"... "better"... to give their attention to.

Do they give even a moment's thought to how this feels to their child? To what this is saying to their children? What example are these parents setting about the value of human interaction? How will these younglings respond later in Life... when their parent wants or needs their attentive interaction? There's even a song about *that*.

Parents will boast about their kids to friends and colleagues... telling them their children are the most important thing in their lives. This doesn't mean their kids ever hear any of that. Based on the way they are actually treated... criticized... neglected... ignored... kids have little evidence to know they are valued by their parents.

A neglected child carries with them these perceptions of unworthiness... subtle and profound... becoming an adult who is easily overwhelmed or discouraged. A person who will discount, neglect or deny their own needs. An adult who believes (unconsciously), "Who I was and what I had to say was not important to my parents... why should what I have to offer now be important to anybody else?" Another Life-constricting false belief.

In my most recent incarnation... I was raised in a home of benign neglect. I wasn't beaten or screamed at... just ignored. Such disregard is a quiet, yet profound, form of mistreatment. Evidently, my dad used to brag about me and my accomplishments to colleagues and neighbors. Or so I heard from them... after he died. He never said *anything* acknowledging to me. As a child, I often felt like a piece of furniture my parents needed to move from Point A to Point

B. A "complication" in the midst of their ever-distracting "more important things."

My kid-self frequently thought... *where's the juicy stuff?*

And yet, blinded by their plight... harried and harassed... many parents don't give "the kids" enough time and quality attention to truly comprehend their amazingness. A great disservice is done. To their kids. And to themselves. Many parents act like hanging out with the kids... or taking care of them... is drudgery. "Let's just slog thru this so we can get on to better... more engaging... more adult things."

And, yes, I know... there is always A Lot To Do. More than likely... as a human adult... especially as a parent... you will be up to your eyeballs in "to do." Getting dinner on the table. Folding laundry. Planning daily Life. Earning money to pay the rent or mortgage. Overwhelm. I am not for a moment downplaying the human adult's ongoing deluge of Life activity.

Yet... even in their down time, many parents are absorbed with their other, "more important" things. From my conversations with Recent Returnees... and my own human experiences... I want to say to you, as you enter this incarnation... if you're going to have kids... be attentive... be engaged. Love 'em up good.

You may recall... when I was here speaking with you earlier... I mentioned a famous book by a children's doctor...

The Common Sense Book of Baby and Child Care. As I noted, the good doctor wrote, "Unless a person has gone thru a significant change in their own consciousness, they will parent exactly the way they were parented."

This brings me to the 2nd parenting observation I have to share with you today. Many children on Planet Earth grow up in difficult... dysfunctional... even horrible... childhood homes and circumstances. As these children grow to adulthood... the pain and fearful limitations of their youngling interactions lead them to 3 different Life choices:

1. I'm sure never going to have children.
2. I had a miserable childhood and I'll be damned if I'm going to give my kid anything better or kinder than what I had to put up with.
3. I am determined to give my children... the love... the caring heart... the fun... the Happy Childhood... I didn't have.

Plan 1 and Plan 3 each offer their own valid options and diversities.

As far as Plan 2... if you *do* have children... just because you had a miserable childhood... do not perpetuate that on your kids. Make that active choice. Don't enable the neglect and abuse to continue. Don't repeat the pattern. As a parent, do everything you can to not be an instrument of the pain you experienced. Take parenting classes. Read books. Observe parents you admire… watch the way they interact with their younglings. Learn. Stretch beyond the way you were parented. Resist becoming the same ol' same ol' you hated. Do better. (If not you, who?) Teach yourself to become a good parent. It is more than worth the effort to be present and engaged in crafting a pleasant, happy home life. Make *those* choices. Healthy for your children. Healthy for your self.

Healthy for parent and child… sets the stage for my 3rd parenting tip. Here is a tool you can use as an adult to release your wounded psyche from childhood mistreatment. It turns out many of the current returnees I spoke with used this technique while in incarnation and found it helpful. Take a moment to activate your Recall + Retain Button so, hopefully, it will occur to you to apply this healing process as you need it while human.

As a human adult, many times as you experience a painful emotion… you can trace it directly to experiencing the same emotional upset when you were a child. When you were a child and pretty much powerless to do anything about it.

Find yourself a quiet place where you can focus your attention. As the adult you are now… allow yourself to feel this painful emotion. Allow your mind to recall a situation where you, as a young child, felt similarly frightened, wronged or upset. You may be surprised how readily these painful childhood memories show up. Looking at this childhood moment in time… allow as many details as possible to fill in the setting. Take the time to feel how your child self was feeling. Be aware of the person or circumstance that was mistreating you. And whoever else may have been there.

As you have the details of the scene and your child-self feelings before you… in your imagination, step into the scenario as the compassionate, caring adult you are now. Confront the situation or person who was mistreating you. Rescue your child self. Show up as the person your child self hoped would come. Save the day! Champion your child self. Be your own defender. Confront the mistreating person… the adult or older child… let them know their time is up. They are outta here! Send them on their way. As your adult self… change the situation so your child self feels safe… acknowledged… valued. Seen. Be a buddy to your younger self. Scoop your little self up in a warm, reassuring hug.

Congratulate your kid self for being brave and courageous.

Having resolved the situation… take your child self out for a really good treat… ice cream comes to mind. Or a toy. Or an adventure. Feel your child self's relief. The wonderment of being rescued. Of being saved… supported… seen. Feel your child self's delight at getting a treat. Let your adult self and your child self *feel* your loving connexion. Savor this marvelous moment.

Applying this healing rescue mission as a human adult, you'll be amazed at the peace… the sense of well-being… it can bring. Generously give yourself this process of transformation… this healing gift… time and again. Relish the experience. You are healing the foundations of your Life.

If you were a lonely or misunderstood child… go to your child self as a kind, encouraging presence. You will feel the deep, peace full effect.

Any adult human will tell you… what happens in your childhood home rides with you… rides on you… for the rest of your incarnation. Be willing and ready to defend and save your child self. You are the Super Hero of your inner psyche.

Being a parent calls you to your highest and best. And it will, again and again. You and your actions… your reactions and responses… your caring and accessibility… are growing the future of humankind.

Be willing to stretch yourself.

I want you to know… I notice an evolution between this visit with you and when I was here before. I see you residing more comfortably in your Tri-Body simulator. You are getting the hang of this human suit. Well-played, my friends. Well-played.

The Interpretorium offers you an incredible opportunity to experience and investigate the interface between consciousness… pure cognitive Love awareness… and this

The Ever-Exhilarating Bliss of Pure Light Consciousness

tri-body instrument you are about to inhabit. Even tho this is a simulation... your rehearsal time here is beyond compare. Experience within these mental, emotional, and physical components... within the actions and reactions... the general commotion of incarnating Human on Planet Earth... will serve you well. These practice sessions offer you a certain sensibility. A knowing. Familiarizing you with ways to best function... in the context of the way things are. You are becoming acquainted... practicing... acclimating... before you hit the ground running.

I know you know, my friends... receiving this opportunity to acclimate = great good fortune.

For eons of time, most beings incarnating on Planet Earth... got born... knocked around a bit... copulated (the show must go on)... found things to eat... figured out how not to get eaten. Then Boom!... right on out of incarnation. That was it. Short attention span theater. Little purposeful guidance was given to soon-to-be-human incarnants heading to Planet Earth. There were no Interpretorium orientation programs. What was the point?

Humans were so totally immersed... riveted deeply within their frazzle and fray. Life on Earth... the density... the distractions... survival (of the fittest and otherwise)... entirely entangled and mangled any human attempts to comprehend higher awareness or to "rise above."

Of course... thru-out time, Earth has, fortunately, had its avatars... teachers... bodhisattvas... messengers. Each having received their own requisite pre-incarnant training and conditioning. But for the most part... the larger numbers of humans did not receive much in the way of pre-consideration or guidance in advance of incarnating on that blue-green orb.

Things have changed. Recognition of Planet Earth's experience sphere evolving... progressing to greater development... calls for more engaged, attentive prep being applied to its incarnating units. This has been true for many hundreds of Earth years. As you look at human history... you see both evidence and effect of this "greater degree of attentive prep." It is evident in the rise and influence of the Greek and Roman philosophers. The mathematics and art of the ancient Chinese and Muslim cultures. The art and architecture... the sculpture and talents of The Renaissance. Human civilization advancing thru... art... music... literature... architecture... mathematics.

Further evidence of more engaged prep is found in the arrival of the Industrial Revolution. Human ideation... building machines to "do the work of men." Invention. Building and productivity greatly multiply. The internal combustion engine. Factories. Electricity... in shops and homes. Refrigeration. "Progress." Society changes.

The concussive effects of the 2 World Wars rips Earth's etheric veils bringing vast change... in hardware and software. A substantial speeding up. For many of Earth's humans, the pace of Life... physically and psychologically... has especially accelerated since the middle of the 20th century. Humankind evolves.

From smoke signals and carrier pigeons to the telegraph... telephones... and now, near-instant communication around the globe. Moving pictures... radio... television... the Internet. Motor cars... airplanes... satellites... spaceships... away out and beyond. Electronics. Computers. Technology. Even more speeding up. The Interpretorium is now in full swing. Far-reaching effort is engaged to prep our Earthtone incarnants. Covering the bases. Let's prepare these incarnating units to a greater degree. Let's get them ready. (As ready as they can be.) We'll bring them up to speed... before they actually incarnate human.

A strategic and necessary design.

I sat where you are now... prepping for my own upcoming human incarnations. I've been here at The Interpretorium trying on my simulant B.E. Suit... marveling. Being able to pre-experience thru this interface... between cognitive awareness and incarnating form... proves itself an incredible assist. As I began waking up in my human

Life... I was increasingly grateful for this pre-incarnate interlude of training and orientation.

Now I'm back here... after spending "decades"... using Earth vernacular to frame time... in a human Life. Juggling all that humans juggle. Juggling is an apt metaphor for humans living Life. Simultaneously, they keep frantic footballs, frosted flakes, and flaming swords a'flyin'. Sustaining in motion all those anvils + hula hoops + blobs of Jello = the reality of human living. Swirling and twirling. Occasionally dropping the ball.

I'll be perfectly honest with you... as much as we create and concoct here in The Interpretorium... there is hardly any effective way to suitably describe humanosity to you as you are sitting here now.

Human Life can be a chaotic circus of lions, tigers, and bears (oh my!)... with a generous share of clowns and miscreant monkeys. Having once again made my way thru it all... I am even more appreciative of the pre-incarnant opportunities made available here in The Interpretorium. Every smidge of incarnation prep proves to be worthwhile.

Interestingly... there are areas on Planet Earth... tribes and territories... which, over millennia, have barely changed at all. Daily Life goes on in these places much as it has since this epoch of human Earth Life began. Other parts of the planet... the "West"... the "developed countries"...

especially big cities... urban areas... offer their own "Life Style"... a multi-faceted way of living. Quite "developed." Quite different... than any way Life on this planet has been lived till now. I mean *really* different.

In many ways, in these "developed" areas... Life is cleaner than it's ever been. In urban areas, humans have tamped down dust and dirt by laying concrete or asphalt over it. And daily Life smells better. This as a result of strategic developments in plumbing structure... both in homes and factories. Pipes are installed underground. Now, there's a good idea! Bringing significant improvements... both in sanitary practices and in more pleasant olfactory exposure. A simple flush will do the job. No more chamber pots to dump and clean. No more nosegays required to sniff as you walk about town.

Oh, and war... make that wars... continue to be *the* go-to population control device on Planet Earth. Along with famine and starvation. Sometimes, famine is an effect of the weather condition called drought... when food-growing areas receive too little rain for food to grow. Many times, starvation is caused by the damage and dislocation of war. War scores big in inflicting human misery.

You may already be aware... Planet Earth's residents continue to be dependent on the burning of fossil fuels to energize their daily living. So quaint. So polluting.

Technologies have been developed to harness sun, wave, and wind power. But humans have not yet made the leap beyond pumping decayed bio-matter to motorize their cars and machinery… to electrify homes and offices. As has been the case since ancient times… humans continue to dig compressed, putrid matter from the earth to heat their housing and generate industrial power. In some rural areas, household fuel continues to be dried animal dung. No digging required.

Currently, there is much debate… dispute… high argument… in the arena of Earth's "developed" societies… as to whether the effects of humans burning copious amounts of fossil fuels are having a harmful impact on the planet's environment and atmosphere. They are. There is ample evidence proving this to be true. Ahhh… but one needs eyes that choose to see. To care.

Said "ample evidence" bumps up against one of the human psyche's favorite, far-reaching fascinations… greed. "What about *mine*?! *My* big pay-off?" "Don't get tricky with new-fangled ideas. I want my consistent, guaranteed income… from the ways things have always been." "Change may affect my bottom line."

The people controlling businesses and corporations… those who profit from the (seemingly) "cheap cost" of continuing to burn fossil fuels… resist and defy any evidence or concern that might attempt to regulate harmful emissions. Their "cheap cost" looks at only current, money-related, bottom-line factors. (*Their* current, money-related, bottom-line factors.) They selectively choose to consider little or none of the related environmental or human "costs." Damages. It has been clearly shown… the concerns of "business" are not the health and well-being of Life. "Business" proves to be concerned only with the perceived monetary effect any attempted regulation might have on the financial bottom line of the few in power.

Short-sighted wins the day. I admit to you… it is easy to become annoyed… exasperated… judgmental… at this self-serving short-sightedness. Truthfully… I admit to being irritated at my own human short-sightedness… as well as that of "others." You will find… many of your fellow humans are driven by a myopic, grasping vision… based squarely on the ol' "I gotta get mine."

And where do you think this short-sighted grasping comes from? Yes, you're right… fear. Fear. There's that BIAS again. As humans insist upon believing, "I am separate from God"… Life is one fearsome endeavor.

This does become tedious to witness.

Deadly tedious. Especially, considered in this context: The "Moon-Oceans-Tidal Trifecta." A Gift to the humans of Earth. To create all the energy they could possibly use, want or need. Hanging on to the "cheap cost" of burning fossil fuels keeps humans grasping and gasping. In the future… harnessing the rhythm of tidal movement will offer a powerful source of abundant, clean energy. Humans have to let go of their near-sighted perception of "cheap and easy" ("Where are *my* dividends?!")… to move beyond "the way it has always been." As humans apply their prodigious cleverness to develop technology utilizing these eternally sustainable resources… energy production will, indeed, be "cheap." Plentiful for all. Life on Planet Earth will change. For the better.

You've probably already heard… both as the result of natural climate cycles and unchecked human emissions… Planet Earth's atmosphere is warming. Glaciers are melting at an alarming rate. This melt adds quantities of water to the planet's oceans. Sea levels rise. Oceans become warmer. Warmer ocean temperatures are harmful to sea Life. Coral reefs bleach and die. Other catastrophes await. The rising sea levels will drown numerous human coastline communities. Both in developed countries… and in subsistence areas where tribes have fished and lived off the sea for generations.

Equal opportunity loss and damage.

Have I mentioned short-sighted?

It's easy to see… as these damaging environmental factors perpetuate… the greatest harm will be to humans themselves. Especially, to the ways humans are accustomed to living. When it comes to realizing how fragile human Life is on Planet Earth... the awareness of humankind seems to be set on "stunted." Willfully blind. "I really don't care, do you?" The frog sitting in the pot of water as it gets hotter and hotter. Welcome to denial.

The human instrument you are about to inhabit is crafted to survive in a particularly limited range of climate factors and conditions. Current short-sightedness does not only pertain to the fragility of the human body. Clean water... clean air... the survival of human food sources... are all even more endangered. As environmental dynamics continue to decline... if the humans themselves don't die off immediately... their food sources certainly will.

I know I'm sounding miffed. Perhaps even alarmist. Having just been there... having just experienced firsthand this willful lack of awareness... it's hard not to be irritated. And alarmed.

I have to say... I find it intriguing these issues of toxic planetary polluting and rising sea levels are coming to a head at the same time humankind is entering its long-awaited epoch of Consciously Evolving Awareness. This short-sighted pollution of air, water, and soil may well bring the end of Life on Planet Earth as humans have lived it for thousands of centuries. As I've mentioned, many mammals will also be affected... along with the oceans' reefs and sea creatures. If humankind were on its toes (chances of that = slim)… efforts to rectify the effects of human-generated pollution would have been taken seriously (and seriously taken) decades ago… starting early in their last century. That didn't happen.

Truly, this *is* a perfect example of the frog sitting in a pot of water with the heat on underneath… not realizing… the water is getting hotter and hotter. Until his "goose is cooked." Frogs and geese and their amphibious and flighted friends are all going to feel the effects of this toxic planetary befoulment.

Just as humans are revving up to enter the realm of Extreme Consciousness Sport, this environmental short-sightedness is going to bring increased struggle and strife. Basic Life elements will be in short supply. Clean water. Clear air. Healthy soil. Human survival is on its way into a much more challenging realm. As I think about it… is "challenging" even an adequate word to describe what is to come?

The very basic Life-sustaining commodity of fresh water will become more precious than oil. And more expensive. Hoarded. Talk about very basic… the air humans (and critters) breathe is becoming increasingly foul. An interesting note… humans have developed ways to filter both air and water to make them more mostly usable. But this is not the case with polluted soil... the medium in which their food is grown. Thinking about the disastrous effects of polluted soil leaves me astonished.

Is this best described as careless foolishness? Or foolish carelessness? Perhaps even more accurate... we have here an ill-advised lack of perception. Reflected in treacherous, inadequate action. (Denial.)

The thing of it is... the mountains will continue to stand majestic on Planet Earth. The deserts... the rocks and wind... the mighty forces will persist. The sun and moon will continue to rise and set.

Humans are creating their own future anguish... struggles... suffering. And quite possibly their own demise. The mind-set of many people currently incarnate can be summed up as... "The environment getting messed up is not my problem. Who cares? I'm not even going to be here for it. I gotta get mine while I can!"

You might or might not be in incarnation as this decline in human habitat becomes more severe. Your great-grandchildren will be there for it. And the generations to follow. Your next Incarnation Human on Planet Earth could set you squarely within the consequences of this needless environmental decline and fall.

Talk about putting things in perspective... if more incarnant Earthtone humans "believed in" reincarnation (now there's a hoot… "believing in" reincarnation… like, "Do you *believe in* breathing?")… perhaps they would be more environmentally inclined to take good care of what they've got. Knowing full well they are going to be back to use it… to live in it… again and again. Alas, this degree of awareness is not the case.

As you will soon be deeply ensconced in all there is to consider and maintain as an adult human… I know you will come to appreciate my earlier juggling metaphors. Juggling all those anvils and blobs of Jello. Toss 'em on up in the air! Keep those flaming swords and awkward-shaped footballs successfully airborne and in movement. Juggling raw eggs and small cacti is also evocative of keeping the many wayward aspects of human Life simultaneously in motion. Let 'em spin!

Just that part… the tossing and juggling part… will keep you well-amused and greatly entertained. And, okay… yes… also feeling pretty fried and a little (or a lot) exasperated.

Remember… you are incarnating on Planet Earth to live a… happy… engaged… fulfilling… human Life. You are incarnating on Planet Earth to be a beacon of awareness and compassion. An instrument of helpful service. Don't let the divisive psycho logical fabrications of your personality obstruct your happiness.

The Ever-Exhilarating Bliss of Pure Light Consciousness

Here's a clue… you serve yourself well to remember this. The construct… the division… between "us" and "them" is a myth. A misguided and misguiding human invention.

Shower the people you love with love. Don't tie your shoelaces together at the beginning of the race by descending into the self-absorbed and judgmental. Be kind. Encourage others. Choose to be amused. Be a friend. See others in a lifted Light. See your self that way. Elevate others with your words and your deeds. With your caring attention.

Draw a deep, centering breath. Thru your Life Time on Planet Earth… do what you can to keep in mind… you are Spirit living a human experience.

Remember.

Hold your focus.
Be of light heart.

Proceed.

CHAPTER TWO

" <u>11</u> "
Maylaigh: The Love That Heals

*"I was reaching for Love.
Where did all this not-Love come from?!"*

I often wish I'd saved the blurb in the Experimental College Catalogue that led me to The Nature of The Soul. I remember the words... "meditation"... "reincarnation"... "karma." Words that made me think... "Ahh... right up my alley." As significant as The Nature of The Soul turned out to be for me... I'd love to see the exact words which intrigued me to the point I actually took myself to that fateful first class. In the spring of 1984... I came across another Life-transforming blurb I wish I'd saved.

I am not a person who often reads the classifieds in the newspaper... maybe 10 times in my adult Life. I don't remember what had me looking thru the classifieds in March of 1984... on what turned out to be a day of auspicious portent. (Who knew?) I do remember reading the ad and getting right up with newspaper in hand to find Scott.

"Listen to this"... I said, as I read the ad to him. We were living in Corvallis, Oregon at the time. A classified announcement in the Corvallis Gazette Times said something like, "How would you like to get together for a long weekend with like-minded people to meditate and share spiritual awareness at a large retreat center house in Southern Oregon? All expenses paid."

Well... yeah. That *does* sound intriguing.

I called the phone number in the ad and reserved a spot for the 2 of us. I mentioned the ad in meditation groups I was leading at the time. Our friend, Jan, who had participated in several of my women's circles... and her husband, Boyd... decided to join in the long weekend, too. Several weeks later... as Isaiah and Lyla spent the weekend with their dad... Scott and I drove to Southern Oregon to be part of this group of like-minded folks.

We arrived late Friday afternoon. It was a big, lovely house out in the country near the tiny Oregon communities of Drain and Yoncalla... south of Eugene. The staff warmly welcomed 16 of us participants. We settled into the bedrooms we were assigned… then came together in the large main room. We introduced ourselves and added our names to teams who would be responsible for making, serving, and cleaning up the meals for the weekend. These food-prep teams proved to be a highlight of the weekend. Pulling the meals together turned out to be much fun… and a good way to get to know the other folks and staff.

The first food-prep team made a delicious dinner. We all sat around a large table eating and talking. After dinner and clean-up, there was an orientation in which we learned we would be divided into 2 groups of 8 people each. There would be a lot of group meditation thru-out the weekend. Sounds good to me.

The next day… after a morning meditation and a talk by our host… we divided into our 2 groups of 8. Scott and I chose to be in the same group. Jan and Boyd were in our group, too. As per instruction… taking turns, one person in the group would deepen into meditation while the other 7 people in the circle asked the meditating person questions.

With each inquiry… the intent was for the person in meditation to be centered… listening within. Encouraged to steer beyond the immediate, knee-jerk, intellect chatter… "I know! I know!" Yes… that very intellect who likes to think it has *all* the answers.

Rather than responding with the first thought that popped up... the person sitting in meditation was to deepen into a place of stillness and *allow the response to reveal itself.* Evolutionary! As you can imagine, this turns out to be a slow, quiet process. The meditator is using a completely different "way" to find an answer.

As I settled into my turn in deep meditation... centering to receive my first question... Jan piped right up, "What is Humanity's next step in Soul growth?" Sitting there with my eyes closed, I thought, "Oh great. *Really?!* Like I would know. That's real light-weight. Is she kidding?!"

Despite my anxious mental chatter... I continued to focus. Quieting. Settling. After several minutes, from a deep, still place came the response:

> "Humanity needs a new word
> for The Love That Heals."

I remember thinking... "Whoa. That's good." As I spoke the response aloud... I relaxed... thinking that was it.

Then Jan asked... "What is that word?"

Oh sure... right. A little exasperated, I thought, "Geez. Well, if I knew..."

I continue to sit. This is a pretty fascinating experience. Reaching into the stillness.

After a bit... I notice a merry-go-round revolving in front of the right side of my forehead. As I start watching it... I see instead of horses riding up and down... there are capital letters riding up and down. As I watch the letters... I see there is an empty space. Then the letters start again.

Starting with the first letter after the empty space comes around again... I spell what I see... "M-A-Y-L-A-I-G-H."

Again, I settle back... thinking, "There... done."

Jan asks, "How do you pronounce it?"

Holy cows! Flipping out a little bit, I'm thinking... "If I *knew* how to pronounce it, I would've told you!"

This is a lot of pressure!

With my eyes still closed, drawing a deep breath, I settle again. Relax. Focus. Exasperation lets go. I listen. In my head I try different pronunciations. After each attempt I get a "Brzzt!"... like a game show buzzer. "Brzzt!... that's not it." After the 3rd inner "Brzzt!"... I draw a deep breath and quiet some more. I hear *may-lay* with a very soft 'kh' sound at the end. I say it in my head a few times. No "Brzzt!" Then, I speak it aloud... "Maylaigh"... May LAY ikh.

Maylaigh is a new word for The Love That Heals.

When I open my eyes... everyone in the circle is looking at me. The expression on their faces says it all. This has been a moment of consequence. Of portent. We all just had a Holy Wow! moment.

I was deeply touched by the experience. (I still am.) The resonant quality... the timbre... the tone... of the whole undertaking. I had been given an incredible gift.

Thinking about it now... I realize the caliber of this experience was similar to the Tuesday Night Hug Scott and I shared. Similar... but different. Definitely an attention-grabber. Sure got *my* attention! Residing in an Amazement Zone all its own.

I will readily admit... Love has always held a certain fascination for me. I am not talking about boyfriend/girlfriend love (which is, of course, engaging in its own way)... or "I love your shoes" love. I am talking about Love that is the force and source of All. As I mentioned earlier... when Lyla was born... the recall information so blew me away the first time I touched her. "*I am going to be your mother!?!*" Was followed by a deep and certain voice... "Yes... for the love."

"Oh... okay. I can do *that*."

As I studied The Nature of The Soul in my early 20s... I was especially drawn to the phrase, "Give me knowledge of the Law of Love." There's a *Law* of Love?!

I would think... *Well, there is a Law of Gravity. If there is a "Law" of Love... it must be as pervasive... as persuasive... as the Law of Gravity.* Which, let's face it, is pretty pervasive. Definitely persuasive. I would sit and imagine experiencing Love in my body just as profoundly as I experienced the force of gravity holding me in place on the planet. A solid, compelling force.

Which would lead me to think... *Where do I go to acquire knowledge of the Law of Love?*

I found out.

The "school" for learning about Love? Your own Life.

There is nowhere better... no greater encyclopedia or "learning environment" than your own choices... your own challenges. Your own relationships. Your own realizations.

Nobody else teaches you about the Law of Love. They may talk about the Law of Love. You may read about the Law of Love. But in reality... this is something you teach yourself. Something you realize yourself. Something you remember you know.

In my early 20s... other than likening it to gravity... I didn't even know how to think about the Law of Love. I had *no* idea how to explore it... how to get to know more about it. It drew me. The Law of Love called to me. I was compelled. What does that *mean*?

Since that auspicious day in May of 1984 when Maylaigh unfolded before us... Scott and I have explored... exercised... and opened to... the cleansing... balancing... awakening...

force of Maylaigh in our lives. Not like every moment of every day. More like when we are able. In amongst everything else... as we're walking around... living Life. We didn't just explore and open to Maylaigh as we sat in meditation. Altho there are times when our understanding of Healing Love has developed in that way, too.

Our "exploration" of The Love That Heals happens more on the fly. In the busy thick of it all. Choosing. As we would think of it. In the midst of navigating the many "activities of daily living." Those compelling realities of Life... our relationship... raising children... working... finances... dealing with the maintenance of the day-to-day. Each of these "activities" alive with their own trials and challenges. When we would remember inside ourselves... in the thick of... the frustrations... the craziness... the difficulties... the laughter. When we were able to... we gave The Love That Heals... possibility. Attention. Presence in our hearts. Space in our minds. In this moment. Here. Now.

Here.

Now.

Compelled as I was... as I am... by The Love That Heals... my explorations began to reveal... there are "stages of development." Hmmmm... interesting. The process... the progress... of Healing Love begins to unfold with Pre-Maylaigh... The Love That Feels.

Gotta get over "not feeling." Definitely gotta get over being terrorized by my own emotions. Gotta get over tricking myself… getting spooked by that ol' Emotional Boogie Man. As I keep myself from running… denying… wishing away my pain. As I choose different… turning to actually look at the turmoil. Interesting discovery… that Boogie Man is a cardboard construct… propped up by 2-by-4s. Flapping around… seeing if he can rattle my cage. Cause a stir. Get me riled up and off center. That Boogie Man counts on me getting snagged by my emotional gyrations. Tangled. Trapped. Consumed.

The Emotional Boogie Man loses his grip… kinda dissolves… when you stop believing in him. Stop believing there is something wrong with you. When you stop getting spooked. When you stop letting him and his wily ways grab your attention and win the day. When you stop being scared of your own emotions. Scared of your own self. Scared of your own Life.

Gently delve into your emotional nature. There's a lot going on in there. No joke. Let's explore. "Hello Emotional Self… what are your gifts for me?" That's a helpful approach. Encouraging. Much more encouraging than a testy, "Why are you always messing with me?!"

Then, there's the ever-intriguing… "What am I going to find out about myself when I get over being afraid to find out about myself?" What, indeed.

Let's begin with a little chaperoned safari into your emotional self. You, in the company of self-kindness. A mighty duo.

Holding hands with self-kindness... agree to take a look around in your emotional nature. A little sightseeing. You don't have to be completely brave. Just willing. Willing to explore. Willing to discover. Willing to learn to be okay with your own fine self.

This *willingness* to explore your emotions... perchance to feel... is Pre-Maylaigh. This is excavation. Cultivation. Turning the soil. Removing calcified inner obstacles on your way to Maylaigh. Allowing The Love That Heals to acquaint you with a kinder, healthier way to engage yourself. Turns out there's more to this emotional evolution than previously realized. Awesome.

Becoming familiar with... embracing... actualizing... The Love That Heals brings your evolving inner Life to Uber-Maylaigh... The Love That Reveals. Reveals? Reveals what? Aha!! The really cool part. Revelation. "That's *me*?!"

Clearly, there is *so much more* to you. Beyond anxiety and upset. Beyond unaware self-limitation and obstacle illusions. So. Much. More.

I only say this 'cause it's true.

(BTW... I came to see this third "phase" as Uber-Maylaigh *long* before the ride-share company came along.

Uber is a German word meaning "outstanding, supreme, above." In this case... "uber" has nothing to do with automotive transportation.)

Making yourself available to this process of Maylaigh is not an intellectual activity.

Exploring The Love That Heals within yourself is unlike any other endeavor.

You are exploring your heart... your emotions... your being... your identity... in a whole new way.

This new exploration of your emotional self means exercising your ability to choose. Choosing to be open to the insight and self-realization The Love That... Feels... Heals... Reveals... has to offer. What might those insightful possibilities be? There is really only one way to find out for yourself. Exploration. Choice. Exercise.

Choosing to look at your Life from a different perspective. Exercising your emotional muscles. Choosing to understand... to be tolerant... of yourself. Of others. Choosing Love within yourself. Expanding your Life possibilities. Exercising more dimensional perceptions. Choosing Love. In this moment.

In this moment, too.

And, again.

What does "choosing Love" mean? Exercise. Choose Love within your heart and mind. Explore. Find out for yourself. Within your thoughts and feelings. Within this moment. How does this feel when I . . . ? Watch for results. Insights. Self-revelation.

You are evolving your human perceptions from Intellect to Intuition. Exercising. Stretching. Exploring. Steps. Along your path. Your possibilities expand. Your identity ignites. A whole new world opens before you. A world rich in increasing awareness.

Many times… externally… your world looks just like it always has. Your view… your perspective… your internal Life is what's shifting. Growing. Glowing.

There is a reason we need a word to mean specifically The Love That Heals. Exactly *that* love.

It has been said the Inuit people of Alaska and the frigid North have a number of words to describe the different qualities of snow. In English… not perceiving the fine nuances… we call it "snow." In English, we have one word… "Love"… which is used to describe the qualities of numerous emotional states. These states range from… "I love your lip gloss!"… to the romantic love a couple shares… to the caring camaraderie of good friends… to parent/child love… to "I love yoga." To the blind, self-serving love of "I love you, therefore you will do everything I want you to do, because I love you."

When considering The Love That Heals… we are not talking about emotional adoration… nor the roller-coaster of romantic love. We are talking about a broad, vast compelling.

Healing Love. Life-transforming Love. Love-transforming Life. Lifting your awareness to greater possibilities Love.

Having this particular word, Maylaigh... a word specifically meaning The Love That Heals... allows you to focus on *that* exceptional force of nature. That specific Life-defining element. That state of vast, dimensional human capability. *That* Love.

The Love That *Heals*.

You may recall from Chapter 7, in Volume II... "healing" does not mean there is something wrong with you... as if you need to be "fixed." Healing doesn't mean you're messed up. Healing means you are embracing your ability to become more awake and aware in your Life. More resolute. Resonant. Radiant.

Awake and aware in this moment. Here. Now.

Healing is a journey. A Life-transforming process. Healing graces your Life as you move from being unconscious to conscious... unhappy to happy. From numb to awake. From apathetic to aware.

Numb and unhappy may feel familiar. But do numb and unhappy make a satisfying Life?

Healing is your process of becoming. Becoming more of your wondrous self.

With this word... Maylaigh... we can work The Love That Heals right on into the conversation. We have a word for it.

As a new word... an inspired word... Maylaigh can mean The Love That Heals in every language. This is not an "English" word... nor an "American" word. Maylaigh is an inspired word. A universal word. Describing a universal state. A vast, universal, perfecto playground.

Now... a person from Scotland can say "Maylaigh" to a person from Tajikistan... and altho they do not share a common language... they would both know they are speaking of The Love That Heals.

Using this word... Maylaigh... allows humankind, each in our own way... to focus on... to open to... that Healing Love. Specifically *that* Love.

"What is Humanity's next step in soul growth?" Humanity needs a new word for The Love That Heals. Maylaigh. Configured by compassion. Designed to remind. To guide. To open... you. To clarity. Insight. Purpose. Your Self. With intention. With love.

Try chanting "Maylaigh." See what happens. Meditate on Maylaigh... The Love That Heals.

In his own meditation, Scott received the chant... "OM Maylaigh OM." Inspired. Our CDs of this chant are well-received. Here's what especially resonates with me about this chant... OM Maylaigh OM effectively merges the ancient, sacred OM... with the new, inspired word for The Love That Heals... Maylaigh.

From humankind's many centuries of sage, centering wisdom... the sacred OM reaches thru the generations... to hold hands with Maylaigh... a new, uplifting realization of the dynamic potential of Love. Awakening to that promise. The vast capacity of Love. Continuing to unfold in human awareness.

Within our human realm... energy follows thought. Turning your attention to The Love That Heals energizes that possibility... that certainty... within your Life. Giving your attention to Maylaigh allows Healing Love to do its Life-transforming work. In you. In your Life. In our world.

Do you remember reading in Chapter 7 about "The Oval of Light?" That quirky Life nuance... (quirky Life nuisance?)... that has you up basking in Radiant Light Essence one minute... and then down floundering in The Poo the next? Sigh.

Here on Planet Earth, polar opposites abound. Earth is not called The Planet of Paradox for nothin'.

Based on that "Oval"... that particular "experience of Life" process... I am going to be straight with you here. As you begin to actively work with The Love That Heals within yourself... there is one thing you can count on happening. Your Life... your thoughts... your feelings... will regale you with... all that is *not* Love.

This will be perplexing. Sometimes devastating. The pain and confusion will certainly prove captivating. "This isn't what I want to happen! I was reaching for Love. Where did all this *not*-Love come from?!"

Wellll... it's been accumulating. In this Life. In past lives. Some of this not-Love you rode into incarnation with... the gyrations of your particular karmic spin. Some of this not-Love rides along with the rodeo. Life factors. Paralyzing parental perspective. Environmental conditioning. Circumstances. Reactions to circumstances.

Many humans grow up convinced... anguish... doubt... rage... harsh self-judgment... is all there is to Life. They greet their Life calcified in defensiveness. Fighting with Life. (Life fighting back.) Snapping others' heads off. Being mean to themselves. Being mean in general. Poor judgment. Their snarling Life-perspective reflects back to them... narrow and unimaginative. Their stance ultimately proving to be both short-sighted and disturbing. Debilitating, even. Exhausting. Certainly misguided.

Plainly put... there are better, more worthwhile things to do with yourself and your Life than being grumpy, short-sighted, short-tempered and transfixed by your poo.

The most worthwhile thing you can do for yourself? Get over being triggered by your poo. It just is. Poo. So what? I know, it's *super* convincing. "I'm Such *Big* Poo! Be terrified of me! Be terrified of yourself!" In truth… it's just a construct. Conceptual elements. Poo charades.

Pain and confusion are big-time players in Earth's paradoxical realm. You may see what hurts you and seems to hold you back. You may get twanged. This does not mean you have to put a long-stem rose between your teeth and tango with your pain.

As Buddha noted… "There is suffering." In offering the venerable Eightfold Path… Buddha proceeded to describe the many capabilities we humans already have to alleviate our suffering. Upon closer examination… more than one of those ways is a Buddha-speak variation of "Let go of your poo."

You may recall… part of The Oval of Light process = you consciously taking Light deep into your inner darkness. In this case… you are consciously taking Love into the places inside you that are not Love. The places in yourself hungering for Love. Hungering for *your* Love. "The reason I am in this dark, difficult place is to bring Love in here." Do just that. Even for a millisecond… a blink. Bring it in. Bring it on. Think "Love." Here. Like for 2 seconds. 5? Maybe 10.

Hold the Light. Shine it on those owie places inside. No fixing or fretting. No angling or analyzing. Just bringing. Just shining. Light.

The Light of Awareness.

Redemption abounds. You redeem yourself. You release yourself from the shackles of self-limiting beliefs. You rise above your guilt, doubt, anxiety, anger. You rise above short-sighted. You lift your Life... your self-perception... into Greater Clear Light Compassion. Grace becomes your accomplice. Your sidekick. Caring... compassion... clear sight... become your posse. Your allies on the Wonder Wheel of Life.

You get over being triggered... flattened by the stupid stuff. You begin to observe the ever-unfolding process that is Life. "Now I see what's mine in this dilemma." "Now I see what's not mine." "I know what to do." "I know what not to do." "I can let this go." "Movin' on."

Ahhhh... More Redeeming.

Your awareness begins to make different choices. Fulfilling, healthy choices. Ultimately... you repurpose the energies ensnared by your self-imposed limitations. You recycle the energy trapped in calcified inner constraints to express as something more functional. More constructive. More effective. More fun.

Energy is always just energy... moving in and out of shape and form. "Energy follows thought" is a profound principle... a foundation in humankind's spiritual traditions. The Book of Proverbs states, "As a man thinketh in his heart, so is he." Our thoughts and beliefs shape the forms Life energy takes in our lives. As author, James Redfield puts it, "Where Attention goes Energy flows. Where Intention goes Energy flows."

You can change the shapes, the contour and terrain of your internal landscape. You choose the form energy takes as it lives in you. Your released Life energies transform… revealing latent, hibernating, Glorious You… at the core of your being.

At our very core… what are we humans becoming? Hopefully, we are lifting our awareness. Growing up. Maturing into more aware beings. Emerging. Not getting twanged so easily. Not falling for it. Not hanging on to the twang. Not believing all that twangs is true.

It is the heart seeking to heal… not hurt… we are each evolving to.

∿ ∿ ∿

In the later '80s, Scott and I were ordained thru the Spiritual Healers and Earth Stewards Assembly (S.H.E.S.) in Seattle, Washington. The next month, I was invited to officiate a wedding. This began decades of delight-filled service and rewarding wordsmith creativity as I performed weddings and created baby blessings… family blessings… house and office blessings… memorial services.

As you know by now… I like words. For each of these different types of Ceremony, I created a resource of written material. Words to grace the moment... for the engaged couple... loving parents... or the tenderly bereaved. Offering this written resource, I say... choose from these words and phrases, these rituals to create your own Ceremony. One that really hums for you. In The Wedding Words and other ceremony possibilities I have devised... many of the words and phrases I wrote myself... others I compiled from a broad range of different sources.

One time, I was invited to perform a wedding at a charming old stone mill in rural Washington State. The mill's water wheel was still intact... little wooden buckets... lifting water from the bubbling stream... tumbling it back out. At the rehearsal, the day before the wedding... I commended the bride on the lovely Ceremony she created. She used some of the offerings from my Wedding Words... also including other lovely pieces she liked. I had a good laugh when, in response to my compliment, without missing a beat, she said... "If you use more than 5 sources, it's research, not plagiarism." Ha ha... good to know.

I especially like performing Vow Renewal Ceremonies. It's says a lot when a couple who has "been around the block" a time or 12... are still so in love with each other... still so value their marriage... they want to acknowledge and recommit to their special bond all over again. A rich, loving experience for the couple and for all who join them to share the moment.

I feel strongly... an engaged couple... or new parents... or bereaved family members... should be able to choose the words that make their Ceremony. If they would like. A couple getting married may feel a strong connection with their religious tradition and want to use words which have been spoken during weddings for centuries. That's fine. And exactly the way their ceremony should be.

But those words and traditions may not have meaning for other couples getting married. When this is the case... the couple should be able to choose Ceremony words that speak to them. Reflecting who *they* are. This is also true of Baby Blessings and Memorial Services.

In The Wedding Words... I have sections with words and phrases for... The Exchange of Vows and Rings... Special Readings... Including Children. I offer Symbolic Ceremonies... such as hand-fasting or a candle-lighting.

Here are a few of my favorite phrases from The Wedding Words... I like to begin with:

FAMILY AND FRIENDS,
WE ARE ASSEMBLED HERE TODAY AND BLESSED WE ARE
BECAUSE IT IS LOVE THAT GATHERS US.
THIS CEREMONY IS AN OPPORTUNITY FOR ALL OF US HERE
TO OPEN OUR HEARTS
TO THE HEALING, JOYFUL, TRANSFORMING POWER OF LOVE.

To the Bride and Groom:

> MAY YOU BE BLESSED, EVERY STEP OF YOUR PATH,
> BY THIS LOVE THAT YOU SHARE.
> MAY THE MIRACLE OF THIS MARRIAGE
> UPLIFT YOUR WELL-BEING
> AND FILL YOUR DAYS WITH HAPPINESS.

> WE WISH FOR YOU A LOVE
> THAT MAKES BOTH OF YOU BETTER PEOPLE,
> A LOVE THAT BRINGS OUT THE VERY BEST YOU CAN BE.
> WE WISH FOR YOU A LOVE THAT GIVES YOU JOY
> AND A ZEST FOR LIVING,
> A LOVE THAT GIVES YOU ENCOURAGEMENT AND SUPPORT
> TO FACE THE CHALLENGES AND RESPONSIBILITIES OF LIFE.

THERE WILL BE THINGS TO BE ANNOYED ABOUT WITH EACH OTHER. AND THERE WILL BE THINGS ABOUT ONE ANOTHER WHICH DELIGHT YOU. DO NOT DWELL UPON EACH OTHER'S FAULTS, BUT RATHER RISE TOGETHER ON THE WINGS OF ACCEPTANCE. REMAIN AWAKE IN TIMES OF ADVERSITY. MAKE USE OF THOSE TIMES AS A MEANS FOR GROWTH AND REALIZATION.

> THE VISION OF YOUR LOVE IS BRIGHT AND CLEAR.
> YOUR SOULS ARE STIRRED TO INSPIRATION BY THIS LOVE

YOU FEEL FOR ONE ANOTHER.
GIVE EACH OTHER YOUR VERY BEST...
AND KEEP THIS LOVE, THIS INSPIRATION,
VIBRANT AND ALIVE.

FROM EVERY HUMAN BEING
THERE RISES A LIGHT THAT REACHES TO THE HEAVENS.
WHEN 2 PEOPLE WHO ARE DESTINED TO BE TOGETHER
FIND EACH OTHER,
THEIR STREAMS OF LIGHT FLOW TOGETHER,
AND A SINGLE, BRIGHTER LIGHT
SHINES FORTH FROM THEIR UNION TO BLESS THEIR WORLD.
THANK YOU BOTH FOR BEING JUST SUCH A BLESSING

Many times, I close a wedding ceremony with these words attributed to Native American traditions:

NOW YOU WILL FEEL NO RAIN,
FOR EACH OF YOU WILL BE SHELTER TO THE OTHER.
NOW YOU WILL FEEL NO COLD,
FOR EACH OF YOU WILL BE WARMTH TO THE OTHER.

NOW THERE IS NO MORE LONELINESS.
NOW YOU ARE TWO PERSONS,
BUT THERE IS ONE LIFE BEFORE YOU.

GO NOW TO YOUR DWELLING PLACE
TO ENTER INTO THE DAYS OF YOUR TOGETHERNESS

> AND MAY YOUR DAYS BE GOOD
> AND LONG UPON THE EARTH.

There are times the bride and groom already have children together... or children from previous relationships. I like including the kids in the Ceremony:

> ALWAYS REMEMBER... YOUR CHILD IS A UNIQUE BEING
> ON THE PATH OF HER OWN DESTINY.
> YOU CANNOT GIVE HER TOO MUCH LOVE.
> YOU CANNOT GIVE HER TOO MUCH STRENGTH
> OF BELIEF IN HERSELF.
> NOR CAN YOU GIVE HER TOO MUCH WONDER
> OF THE WORLD AROUND HER.

> THESE ARE THE CERTAINTIES THAT WILL SUSTAIN HER
> IN A SOMETIMES DIFFICULT WORLD.
> GIVE HER THE GIFT OF HUMOR.
> GIVE HER THE GIFT OF MUSIC.
> GIVE HER THE GIFT OF BELIEF IN HER OWN CREATIVITY.

For younger children, it is nice to include a gift for them... a watch, a necklace, a bracelet or ring:

> THE RINGS THAT OUR BRIDE & GROOM
> GIVE THEIR CHILDREN TODAY
> ARE TO SAY...
> WE ARE NOW A FAMILY.
> THE 4 OF US ARE A GIFT TO EACH OTHER.

YOU ARE EACH A BLESSING TO THIS FAMILY.
FROM THIS DAY FORWARD,
IT IS YOUR PRIVILEGE AND JOY TO BE WITH EACH OTHER
AS YOU GROW AND LOVE TOGETHER.

(The words "bride and groom" or "their children" are changed in the Ceremony to their own names. I print the service in CAPS to make it easier for me to read during the Ceremony.)

Sometimes, in either a wedding or a baby blessing, I include all or part of the poem, "Just Like You" written by the prolific American poet, Edgar Guest. Mr. Guest was popular in the first half of the 20th Century… known as "the people's poet." Here is an excerpt from his insightful poem:

THERE ARE LITTLE EYES UPON YOU
THEY'RE WATCHING NIGHT AND DAY
THERE ARE LITTLE EARS LISTENING
TO EVERYTHING YOU SAY

THERE ARE LITTLE HANDS ALL EAGER
TO DO EVERYTHING YOU DO
AND LITTLE PEOPLE WHO ARE DREAMING
OF THE DAY THEY'LL BE LIKE YOU.

THERE ARE WIDE-EYED LITTLE PEOPLE
WHO BELIEVE YOU'RE ALWAYS RIGHT

AND THEIR EARS ARE ALWAYS OPEN
AND THEY LISTEN DAY AND NIGHT

YOU ARE SETTING AN EXAMPLE
EVERY DAY, IN ALL YOU DO
FOR THE LITTLE PEOPLE WHO ARE WAITING
TO GROW UP JUST LIKE YOU.

The following are a few resonant phrases for a Memorial Service:

TODAY THE PRESENCE OF EACH ONE OF YOU HERE
IS A LOVING ACKNOWLEDGEMENT
OF THIS VIBRANT WOMAN'S LIFE.

ALTHO SORROW AND LOSS CAN BE
ALL-CONSUMING AT TIMES...
WE MUST AFFIRM THAT THE LIFE COURSING THRU US
HAS PURPOSE BEYOND SORROW.

THE ALCHEMICAL CHANGES POSSIBLE
THRU THE GRIEF PROCESS...
WILL TOUCH EVENTS IN YOUR LIFE WITH MEANING...
AND CONFIRM THE PRECIOUSNESS OF YOUR OWN LIFE.

TODAY SHE GIVES YOU YET ANOTHER GIFT...
ALLOW YOUR REMEMBERING OF HER
AND YOUR SADNESS AT HER PASSING...

TO REMIND YOU…
BE MORE JOYFUL IN YOUR OWN LIFE.

DEVELOP A PERSPECTIVE THAT APPRECIATES
YOUR LIFE AND THE PEOPLE IN IT.
DO NOT BE UPSET BY EVERYDAY ANNOYANCES
AND TAKE THEM SO SERIOUSLY.

SAVOR THE JOYS… THE BEAUTY… THE GIFTS…
OF YOUR OWN LIFE.

I like the phrase… the reminder… "the alchemical changes possible thru the grief process will touch events in your Life with meaning… and confirm the preciousness of your own Life." "Alchemical changes" is a good way to put it.

The very nature of alchemy is transformation. Ancient alchemists strived to purify and mature certain base metals… looking to transmute them into gold. Physical alchemy implies altering… transforming… the properties of matter. Spiritual alchemy is the transformation of your inner Life… your conscious awareness.

In the midst of an experience as profound as grief… there isn't any healthy way to ignore it… or intellectualize your way around it. Stirring the very depths of your being… emotional alchemy is occurring. Changing you. Calling you onward.

"Alchemical changes" also prove to be available within many of Life's profound disappointments and regrets.

Have you noticed... it takes a serious "Whack!" in your Life to "get your attention?" A "Whack!" that sits you right down and makes you look at your self... and your Life... and "things"... differently. As with so many aspects of Life... once you are "sitting down" (willing to pay attention)... the choice as to what happens next is completely up to you. Shall I feel bruised and abused... bitter... shut down... resigned... vengeful? Shall I look around and find... "ways"... "changes"... that will bring me to a more profound understanding of my self and my Life?

Because we are human... a good, solid whack is often what it takes to put our feet on our Path to Awakening.

Ask anyone you know who is alive in their spiritual Life... how did you begin your journey? What led you to become more awake and aware? Invariably... their story begins with mourning some Life calamity. A whack.

This is certainly true for me. As I mentioned in Chapter 1... I'd begun meditating twice a day (having no idea what I was doing)... just a few months before my first husband, Bob, let me know he was in love with another woman. Whack! *Yeow!*

As you can imagine... that is a moment I vividly remember.

We were standing in our living room when he told me. Listening to what he was saying… taking it in… the eye of my mind filled with black silhouettes of skyscrapers falling and crashing against a cantaloupe-colored sky. I was staggering inside. Reeling at this unexpected revelation of betrayal.

As the skyscrapers crashed in my inner vision … outside of my head… above and in front of my right eye… there was a brilliant white point of light… diamond bright. And a voice. Saying… "Everything is going to be alright. Everything is going to be fine."

That seemed highly unlikely.

What a juxtaposition of reality! Black skyscrapers crashing, falling… a voice saying "everything is going to be fine."

Thus… with little fanfare (beyond the crashing skyscrapers)… began the most excruciating period of my sweet, short Life.

Bob and I had been together for one quarter of my Life. I was Bob-and-Dana. I thought we were building a Life together. All of a sudden, he wanted to be with someone else. He alluded this was possibly "just a fling" and, ultimately, he and I would stay together. Oh yeah, like that makes this all so much better. It was clear to me… and my tender heart… his way of being in our marriage was not going to work for me.

A month before Bob dropped his bombshell... my mother attended her monthly gathering of professional women. For their evening's presentation a well-regarded local psychic named Ruth spoke and shared her revelations. Later in the evening, Ruth came up to my mother and said... "You have a daughter." "Yes I do." Ruth proceeded to tell my mother about me. Everything she said was accurate. She told my mother there was trouble in my marriage. My mom could hardly wait to tell me.

Neither of my folks really liked Bob. Nor were they keen on us getting married so young. Understandably, they didn't like that I dropped out of college to support us while Bob continued going to school. My mom didn't exactly clap her hands with glee as she said Ruth told her there was trouble in our marriage. But she sure was smiling. Even a little smug. At the time... as far as I knew, we weren't having marriage problems. Turns out Ruth knew more than I did.

After Bob's admission... I was devastated. Laid low. Seriously adrift. Life as I knew it was smashed to bits. In desperation, I got Ruth's phone number and called her. "Can I come see you?" She remembered her conversation with my mother and immediately invited me to her home. She and I had a powerful connexion... and an extraordinary evening together. Ruth told me many things I had no idea about… regarding my Life and past relationships. Later… as my Life unfolded… everything she told me proved to be true.

Her advice about my current situation? "Leave Bob while the pudding is still warm." While we were still somewhat friendly. She said, "Find your own place." Then proceeded to tell me 6 things about my new place and how I would find it. Three of the items she mentioned I had control over… 3 of them I did not. They all came true.

She told me… "You'll be able to walk to work." Ok. Here's one of the aspects I could control. Driving thru the neighborhood near the bank I worked at… I saw a sign… "1 bedroom apartment for rent." I called the phone number and made an appointment to see it.

Ruth told me I would know the person I rented my new place from (this did not seem likely)… and I would get it for a very reasonable price. Swell!

I arrive to look at the apartment… oh, good golly! The owner is a customer I'm friendly with at the bank! Now there's a pleasant surprise! I checked out the apartment. "I'll take it." The owner proceeded to knock several hundred dollars off the rent… because he liked me and knew I was going thru a difficult time. So, right there… 2 things I had no control over which Ruth was completely accurate about. This seemed to bode well.

I will credit Bob... as soon as he told me about his infatuation... as the silhouette skyscrapers were crashing in my head... he said, "You're going back to school." He acknowledged it had not been "fair" that he continued in school while I had quit to support us.

As we slogged thru our last few months living together... I was also in the process of re-enrolling in college. Bob found a part-time job and went to school part-time. I started working Monday-Wednesday-Friday at the bank and going to school Tuesday and Thursday. There I was, wildly juggling... moving into my own place... working... school. All with a broken heart. In shambles. This proved to be a heavy load. I started thinking maybe I should let go of school.

When I first visited Ruth... it came up in conversation I had a book she'd been wanting to read. I told her I would bring it by for her. The afternoon I was taking the book to her house... I'd had a particularly rough day at school and decided I was going to chuck it. As I stepped onto Ruth's porch, she came to meet me at her screen door.

"I have someone here right now Dana, I cannot invite you in."

"That's okay. Here's the book you wanted." I turned to leave.

As I walked down her front steps, she called out... "Don't you dare quit school!"

I stayed in school. A month or 2 later I came across the Experimental College catalogue with the listing for The Nature of The Soul. I didn't put it together right away... but when the realization struck, I wondered... did Ruth tell me, "Don't quit school!" because she sensed something monumental was on my horizon? A monumental something which would come to me because I was in school? I won't ever know. Experiencing Ruth's perceptions... her "sight"... as I had... this certainly seems likely.

And the years fly by...

Oh those flying years. The movement of time strikes the different generations of humankind differently. It is as if the generations on Planet Earth look thru opposite ends of the same time-based telescope. As tho younger folks are looking thru the end that makes things look small and far away. Gazing 50 years into the future... the distance... the passage of *that much* time... is nearly unimaginable. So far away. Such an incredibly loooong time. Elders... having lived those 50 years... view thru the other end of the telescope... the end that makes everything appear closer. Memories and feelings are fresh. Close. They see their years passed as if they were yesterday. "That was hardly any time at all." Those 50 years shot by in a flash. Blink! Ahhh... perspective. Life.

Thru the '90s, our family... Scott, Isaiah, Lyla, and I... were involved with the congregation at Unity of Beaverton.

I was the Women's Minister. Scott was the Prayer Team Minister. Lyla, in her early teens, was asked by Rev. Ed Townley, the Senior Minister, to team with an adult volunteer, Andrea, to start a Youth of Unity (Y.O.U.) chapter for teens at the Church.

It was slow going at first. But Lyla and Andrea stuck with it… meeting together on Sunday mornings. Fortunately, they enjoyed each other's company. Eventually, teens did start showing up. After a few months… this group really took off. In being willing to create the space for this Y.O.U. group… Lyla served both the Church Family and the teenagers of the local community. Y.O.U. at Unity of Beaverton has well-served many teens and their families over these past 20 years. I am proud of Lyla for saying "Yes"… and making it happen.

※ ※ ※

Scott and I went thru 4 scorching years in the mid-90s… in our relationship… in our Life in general. Here is something we learned quite unexpectedly. Out of all of the insight and awareness that came our way thru this difficult time… this was the most humbling. And, as I said… most unexpected.

As the Prayer Team Minister… and the Prayer Team Minister's wife… Scott and I were at the church every Wednesday evening and every Sunday after the morning

Service... to reach into The Prayer Box and pray for the well-being of others. Many times, different members of the congregation joined us in the chapel to pray. Sometimes, it was just me and Scott. We would open the prayer box... hold each prayer slip in our hands... and speak aloud a healing prayer for each request in the box.

Neither of us looked for any kind of "benefit" or "reward" to come our way as a result of this. It was simply what we were doing and where we were showing up on Wednesdays and Sundays. We each appreciated these times to be still and prayerful... making space in the midst of the grim, grueling grind that was our Life at the time.

As the months went by... we each sensed the quietly profound impact this activity of praying for others was having in our own lives. The only way I can think to describe it... it felt like a "get out of jail free" card. Altho I could not have told you this at the time... we were each experiencing a variation on the "alchemical changes" I mentioned earlier. No question about it.

Twice a week, we were stepping beyond our own disgruntled feelings to hold another person's challenges in prayer. Moving out of our own difficulties long enough to show up... to be present for others. This did, indeed, have an "alchemical effect." Our lives were touched in unanticipated ways.

Thru The Nature of The Soul, I heard the phrase... "Humanity is served thru imperfect vehicles." I remember thinking at the time... "Good thing, that." The upshot being... don't wait 'til you are feeling all perfect to reach out to help another person. As Scott and I fulfilled our Prayer Team responsibilities... emotionally, we were the most ragged, the most jagged either of us had ever been. But we kept showing up. We kept holding other people's challenges in the Light of prayer.

As I write this, I clearly see... similar to "I can't say exactly what the hypnotherapy sessions worked in me"... I can't say exactly what praying for others did for us at the time. Alchemy... and its "seemingly magical process of transformation"... was having its effect. We both acknowledge those prayer-full experiences as a significant healing factor in our ability to remain together as a couple. At a point when we were hanging on by a thread.

As I look at this now, I can see... speaking healing prayer on behalf of other people in pain was "heart yoga." We stretched. We centered. We acknowledged the Light. And held it. We created a heart-centered container for healing energy. This was in no way intellectualizing. It was an opportunity for each of us to reach outside of ourselves... twisted and troubled as we were... to be present for the well-being of others. We showed up twice a week to honor our commitment to our Church Family. We could not have anticipated the healing effect... the gift... this would bring us.

Another "gift" of unexpected humbling arrived during this time. Just in case we thought things could not get any more intense... in September, 1995... right in the thick of our difficulty and despair... I was diagnosed with breast cancer.

As this was unfolding... for me, personally, this "new wrinkle" was not even "the worst thing" happening in my Life. The hardest things for me were the ongoing thorny issues... the strain and troubles... between me and Scott.

After my diagnosis had been confirmed... I had them biopsy me twice... as I left the doctor's office, I looked up at the sky and said out loud, "You've got to be kidding me." Turns out... not even a little bit of kidding was going on.

October 31, 1995, found me in the hospital having my right breast amputated. Nobody's idea of a good time. In my capacity as the Women's Minister at Unity of Beaverton... I wrote the following for the congregation's monthly *Spirit Expressing* newsletter. I titled it "Choosing Love Over Fear."

On October 4, 1995, I was diagnosed with breast cancer. This diagnosis came as a complete shock. As I was leaving the doctor's office, I laughed out loud, and looking Heavenward said aloud, "You have got to be kidding me!" As this news was sinking in, foremost in my mind was a story I had heard in church when I was 12.

The minister told us of a monk tending his garden. An agitated man came running up to his gate and cried, "What would you do?! What would you do, if you knew you only had an hour to live?!"

The monk paused, reflected, and said, "Tend my garden."

That story, that stance—which had touched me when I first heard it—now, 34 years later, was to serve me well. As I "tended my garden," I continued to lead meditation groups. I went to work. I arranged the bone scan and other hospital tests around the two Wednesday night meditations I had scheduled here at Unity. What else was there to do?

The biggest "glitch" for me, the first few days after my diagnosis, was talking to others about it. I had always been one who, when deeply immersed in my process, my edge, doesn't talk about it. When I have a little distance from the intensity of the issue, I can talk about it just fine. But when I'm right in it, mum has been the word.

Well, that particular personal pattern was about to change, big-time. The Saturday morning after my diagnosis, I was walking one of our dogs and a voice said in my head, "Dana, now is the time to talk about it."

A few minutes after I returned home from that walk, the phone rang. It was Beth Noelle calling to thank me for a card I had sent her. When we had finished that part of the conversation, I forced myself to lurch over a threshold inside and, prying my mouth open, I said, "I have something to tell you."

The result of me speaking my deep, vulnerable edge (telling her of my diagnosis) was spending the rest of that Saturday in the warm companionship of Beth, her husband Scott, and their friend, Khan Majeed. That afternoon, I experienced a pranic healing session with Khan that was profound and insightful.

That has been the wonder of these last 2 months: very difficult and quite blessed, pain and insight, trauma and clarity, worst and best, torture and grace. Just like Life, only more so.

Since 1982, in my personal practice, I have been, whenever possible, choosing love over fear. As I went thru this experience of being diagnosed with cancer, I felt as if I had been working out with emotional barbells for 13 years, strengthening myself to choose, choose, and choose again thru this current challenge of my Life. Choose love, choose trust, and choose love some more.

It is not that I didn't experience fear. I have truly run the gamut of emotion. I feel I have been more awake and aware thru this process than at any other time in my Life. I know I have choice, and I choose love over fear.

> Words that serve me well to remember
> to pry off fear and concern:
> "Worry is interest paid in advance on
> a debt you may never owe."

As I moved thru this incredible time of transformation, I could imagine some people sadly shaking their heads: "Poor Dear, she's in denial." Which they can think, if that serves them well. What I know for me is that I am in MY process. I am experiencing my breast cancer my way. The way that makes the most sense to me. The way that is the most alive to me.

During a healing session, my good friend Rena Davis said, "Dana, this cancer is taking you out of your body." I said, from a deep awareness within me, "No, Rena, this cancer is taking me INTO my body." And that is what is true for me.

The morning I was to go for the bone scan and other tests, I was feeling particularly vulnerable and off-center. I sat at my desk, casting about for some piece of insight that would help me to ground. I picked up an envelope that I knew held a card that Leola Freeman had given me at our Monday night women's meditation group, 2 days before the fateful mammogram.

I had appreciated the card when I received it, but this particular morning, as I took it out of its envelope, on the front of the card, as if anew, I read these words,

"I am centered in my private unfolding.
Aligned with the rich, cool balance of the moment.
I connect to my personal oasis."

What grace! I felt as if the voice of God had whispered in my ear, "Truly, Dana, this is YOUR personal unfolding. Hold your center, be in the moment. Choose love over fear. Trust the perfection of your process." The words from the card became my mantra.

That day, as I went to the hospital for my tests, I was blessed to be accompanied by Susee Ruben and Linda Waltmire. I deeply appreciated their gentle & supportive companionship. We enjoyed a lovely and loving day together, sitting at the hospital, having lunch at Old Wives Tales, walking at Bishop's Close.

As we returned to the hospital for the bone scan, Susee said to me, "Dana, I didn't know this could be this way."

I said, "Susee, I don't know any other way to do it."

There are no "shoulds" about how breast cancer (or any other life trauma) is to be dealt with. What it is, how it is, is how it is for <u>you</u>. The value, the experience, is in how it is unfolding for <u>you</u>.

A frequent response to difficult Life situations is to think, "What did I do wrong?" It is limited thinking to think in terms of "wrong." This is not to say that I do not feel I have areas of negativity that might (or might not) have generated cancer in my breast. I admit to imbalance within myself. I certainly am quite familiar with the breadth and dimensionality of my dark side.

It is not a question of what did I do wrong, but what is my Soul's intent? What is the gift here?

It is a human tendency to judge "good" and "bad." In truth, what is happening simply <u>is</u>. We are given infinite choice as to how we are going to interpret our experiences. It is thru our interpretations that we convince ourselves what is happening, what is real.

That has been one of the true gifts of years of meditation for me—developing the observer, the point of objectivity that can look at Life and see what <u>is</u>. The observer balances our human tendency to judge "good" or "bad," "yikes" or "yum." Without heaps of reaction and emotional gafluffle, it just is what is.

Fran Lancaster sent me a card in which she wrote, "I see a great merging in consciousness as Christ penetrates every thought, feeling, belief, and attitude... releasing the full light you are." As I read her words I thought, "Thanks, Fran, so do I."

I am deeply touched by the love, the care and concern, the food, the flowers, cards, and phone calls that have been sweetly showered upon me by my spiritual family, my tribe, here at Unity of Beaverton. I know that one reason I had no pain in the days after the surgery is because of the prayer energy that was generated on my behalf. And I thank you all so much. My surgeon commented that she felt I had had virtually no pain because of my mental attitude. In response I said, "And the prayers."

As well as the prayer focus here at Unity of Beaverton, I was held in prayer in fundamentalist prayer chains. I was held in prayer thru Silent Unity and Science of Mind. And I know I have done as well as I have physically because of that prayer support. I begin chemotherapy (once every 3 weeks for 6 months) on Dec. 7. Again, I know that your prayers and caring will be with me and see me thru. And again, I thank you.

My Life now has another "marker," another event that stands above the day-to-day—before October 4 and after October 4. When I remember something, or I am somewhere I was before, I think, "Oh yeah, that was before the diagnosis." I now look at my Life and at myself differently. Life is more poignant, precious, and powerful. Paradoxically, I feel more alive(!). And I have a richer appreciation for the knowing that right now is a gift, that is why it's called the present.

I was sent home from the hospital a couple days after my mastectomy... adorned in drainage tubes and reservoir pouches... all requiring frequent care and attention. I was mentally foggy and easily got light-headed. I felt I'd been sent home a few days too early. As we now have accountants and finance in charge of America's healthcare system... instead of healing professionals... I'm sure many people feel they are sent home too early.

At home... there was little respite from the emotional difficulties of the past couple years. The stress... the "ill"... between me and Scott continued, thick and heavy. I was in despair. *This does not feel like my Life.* Being back in it all... an "all" which now included dealing with tubes and pouches and "drainage"... was an oppressive weight. Heart ache. I felt squashed flat. Barely able to draw a breath.

The 3rd day I was back home...I was sitting in our living room... staring off into space. It was gray, cold, and miserable outside. This well-matched the gray, cold, and miserable I felt inside. All of a sudden... from out of nowhere... a voice in my head said, "I trust this blessing."

You say *what*?!

My Life did not look like a blessing. It did not feel like a blessing. It didn't even smell like a blessing.

The moment I heard that voice... I knew what it was offering me. I said, "Yes." I trust this blessing.

In that moment... wretched as I felt... I *knew*... there is blessing here. I did not feel blessed. But I *knew*. There *is* blessing here. And I trust it. I *trust* this blessing.

This was not intellectualizing on my part. I wasn't being all analytical and thinking it over. I just knew. This is true. I may not be able to see it or feel it right now. But I do *trust*. This. Blessing.

I've mentioned before... when Life is rugged... hard... roughing us up... our thinkery goes to stinkery. "My Life is always going to hurt this much." "I am always going to be this miserable." "Things are never going to go right for me."

I've learned from experiences thru-out my Life... this simply is not true. Life does not have to stay stinko. Life isn't even particularly inclined to stay stinko. I knew even in this harsh, difficult time... stinko did not have to win. There *is* blessing here. Even if I am not seeing it. Even if I'm not feeling it right now.

"I trust this blessing" became my mantra. My put-one-foot-in-front-of-the-other-and-just-keep-going mantra. I'm not going to tell you I clicked my heels... shouted for joy... and everything was groovy. It wasn't. Everything just kept grinding on as it had been. But I was in a different place inside. Again... not all golden poppies and sunbeams. But not in such profound misery. The despair did not have the stranglehold on me it had before I heard that voice... those words. That possibility.

I've got to say... I am grateful that in that moment... marinated in the deep misery of those days... as I heard that voice... as I heard that reference to "trust"... that reference to "blessing"... I was able to say, "Yes." I was able to agree. *I may not see it. I may not feel it. But I do trust this blessing.*

Life went on. After 10 days... the drainage tubes and reservoirs were removed. A huge relief. A giant step toward "normalization." Of course... "normal" was not going to be "the same." I did, after all, have a long, flat scar where my right breast used to be. That takes some adjusting to.

I do have to credit Scott... even tho things were so bleak between us... so strained... he never once made me feel ugly or disfigured. I am truly grateful for that.

I eventually returned to work... which included a 25-minute bus ride each way... to and from downtown Portland. I continued to "work with" I Trust This Blessing.

Keeping that door open. Keeping myself available. Respect. First hearing those words opened a door in me. Allowing me to see... reminding me... there are possibilities beyond misery and sadness.

You may remember... my "etheric pouch" at the top of my right thigh. The pocket I've put "pieces of the puzzle" in my whole Life. Well, I also use this pouch to store insights and queries. I would "pull these out" at odd moments... like 25-minute bus rides... to look at and ponder.

Over a year after I first heard "I trust this blessing"... I was riding the bus to work one day, as I'd done so many times before. Sitting there on the bus... I pulled "I trust this blessing" out of my etheric pouch. As I was "looking at it"... contemplating... for the first time it occurred to me to ask... "Just what *is* this 'blessing' I am 'trusting'?"

Ohhhh. Good question.

The answer came immediately. "The blessing is being here."

I was stunned. Here? Being *here*?! Here being *human*?

"The blessing is being here."

Whoa.

Talk about "opening a door!" Sitting there on the bus... a cascade of awareness filled my mind. Dana... beings actually line up to be able to incarnate Human on Planet Earth. Beings actually *want to* be here!

Okay. This is going to take some adjusting to.

I sat on the bus thinking... we humans get so stuck on all the difficulties... why would we ever *choose* to take all this on?! The blessing is being *here*? This was almost more than I could wrap my brain around. *Here?*

Riding this train of thought took me to... I'm sure you've heard people say, "This is my last incarnation"... like it's some badge of honor. "I have it so together in this Life... I won't have to come back here again." Really? Hearing this, I would think... but what about the *bodhisattvas*?

In the Buddhist tradition... a bodhisattva is a person who has achieved enlightenment. Yet... instead of passing from this world to "higher realms"... the bodhisattva makes a conscious choice... a vow... to return to being human.

Returning to this world... time and again. This is a choice. An act of wide compassion. To relieve human suffering. The bodhisattva vows to be in this world... a part of it all... until each human being has attained enlightenment. In the family of Humankind... the bodhisattva is the devoted, enlightened workhorse. Presence. Blessing. Here for us. As we each transform. As we each rise to our very best. As we each do our part transforming human awareness.

The bodhisattva is not one to jabber on about "This is my last human Life."

"The blessing is being here" flung open all sorts of doors and windows in my awareness. Fresh air came streaming in. Along with this came a companion piece of insightful information... "There are so many beings wanting to incarnate human on Planet Earth... a lottery system has been instigated to assure fair and impartial access." Really? A lottery? Intriguing. (Who knew?)

I began looking at Life here on Planet Earth thru different eyes. Beings really *want* to be here?! I *wanted* to be here?! Go ahead... hold this one in your awareness for a while. I *wanted* to be here. One amazing concept to contemplate.

Human Life looks way different from this perspective.

It is A Blessing to be here. A Blessing to be human. "But what about all the stuff I'm upset about!" "What about Life being so hard?" "What about how much I don't want to be here?"

What about it?

Several years before this... I had devised The Interpretorium as the place beings who are out of incarnation would visit... to prepare... to practice... as they are heading into a human Life. This new realization... "We *want* to be here?!"... this new perspective... really put a fresh spin on that ball.

> "I trust this blessing."
> What is this blessing I am trusting?
> "The blessing is being here."

These realizations came my way over 20 years ago. My inner workings have not been the same since. I see this world much differently than I did when I was still objecting to being here. When my little emotional tea bag was still steeping in whining and complaint.

You can fuss and complain about Life... or you can embrace and contribute to Life. What you see *is* what you get. Energy *does* follow thought. The time will come when you perceive your Life as A Blessing. This is exactly when you will *receive* your Life as A Blessing. Which is the awareness destination we are all heading toward.

You make the choice.

Pack your bags of woe and worry... complaint and objections. And toss 'em. They are *not* serving you well. Out goes grievance and grumble. They only weigh you down. Let 'em go, already.

Steer yourself toward seeing and embracing the Good in Life. The Good in yourself.

If not you... who? If not now... when?

This is a choice... a decision... only you can make. It is inevitable.

Don't look back... that's not the way we're going.

Looking back usually focuses on pain and disappointment. How we've been hurt. What we've lost. That's not where we're going. Hanging onto all that regret only weighs you down. It doesn't help you. It only hurts you.

Allow the past to be in the past. Face forward. Look ahead. Proceed.

Your consciousness is evolving in the direction of awakened awareness. Service. Self-kindness. Love. Vast and wide. That's where we're heading.

Repurpose your woe. Deflate your anguish. Recycle your doubt. Release uncertainty. Disentangle from cynicism.

Adapt. Adjust. Attune.

Your energies trapped in these emotional cul-de-sacs need to be repurposed. Want to be repurposed. *Want* to assist… to contribute… to participate… in your awakening.

> Your awareness is evolving to Love.
> Help it along.
> Embrace the process.
> Be an active part of your own uplifting becoming.
> Ride that train.
>
> After all…
> The Blessing *Is* Being Here.

CHAPTER THREE

" <u>12</u> "
The HazMat Variety Show

"I'll take Door #2, Johnny."

Welcome back to your Orientation Moment here at The Interpretorium. Thank you all for arriving in such a timely manner. I commend you for adjusting to the human construct of "time" and "keeping track" of it. Once you learn to decipher them… these "watches" do prove to be useful time-keeping devices.

Depending on your incarnant locale… where on Planet Earth you actually find yourself living Life… you may be vastly engaged with clocks and watches and "keeping track of time." Whereas… living in other locales… you may never lay eyes on a watch or a clock. You will still "keep track of time"... but you'll use different units of measure. Moon cycles. Solstice/Equinox. Sunrise/Sunset. Still "watching time." Just not watching a watch.

As I was out and about, I saw some of you chatting with our Recent Returnee on the sandy beach at Tropix, our little Tiki bar. Isn't she fascinating? So wise in the ways of Earthtone humanosity. And she knows full well the significant role her post-incarnant insights play in these Orientation Moments. She is quite a being. Having incarnated human many times... she is exceptionally well-equipt to acquire notable perceptions while incarnate. In turn, providing you with useful, current information from her most recent human Life. She might have mentioned... she also activates on other planets which include the Human Life Format. Altho, I do happen to know... Planet Earth, with all of its possibilities, nuances and complexities... is her favorite. Totally understandable.

I see some of you in this Orientation Pod signed on to have your Dharmic Sequence Factors calibrated so you, too, will fulfil the prerequisites to become a Recent Returnee. Thank you. I admire your long-term realization goals and your willing service to help others as they prepare to incarnate.

And now... are you ready to receive more fascinating factoids about living human Life on Planet Earth? I'm sure, by this point, you have heard Life on Earth referred to as

The HazMat Variety Show. Sometimes, this is acknowledged with admiration... how do they *do* that?! Other times, it is muttered with scorn... why do they *do* that?!

The HazMat designation refers particularly to the hazardous mental and emotional reactive materials on Planet Earth. Rage. Vengeance. Hatred. Greed. Corrosive and toxic. Each and all.

And, of course, there are the risky physical elements... explosives... radioactivity... poisons. If not handled with the necessary precaution protocols... all of these various materials... vengeance and hatred... explosives and poison... pose a danger to the living of human Life.

There are those who disapprove of Earth's volatile assemblage of miscellanea. They find it disturbing... distorting... delusional. Some are quick to judge Earth's modus operandi as too much of a conglom of insanity... and inanity. "The HazMat Variety Show on Planet Earth?! Honestly! Why even bother going there?"

On many of the planets hosting human variables... Life is a homogeneous study in similarity... similar thoughts... feelings... attitudes... activities. Seen as the goal? Service to the community as a whole... and to well-being in general. These are environments in which much good can be achieved. With a minimum of drama and chaos.

Then there's Earth. The ol' sticky wicket.

Many eons ago... truly, it began as a generous offer... kind of a science experiment. The Planetary Logos of Earth agreed to act as a receptacle for myriad levels of consciousness from assorted Planetary Systems. All at the same time.

It began as an experiment in simultaneous human hodge-podge. Bring it! *All* kinds of consciousness. Avatars. Pirates. Sages. Showgirls. Businessmen. Banditos. Influencers. Comedians. All sorts of acting out and whoop-dee-doo. Comings and goings. Hither and thither. Nearly unimaginable at the time. Sometimes... nearly unimaginable now. All this cavorting requires a lot of sorting.

There are many who would say this gambit paid off.

And, there are still those who disapprove and grumble about Earth.

Not to be ignored... there are many pre-incarnants who are drawn to this blue-green Planet of Paradox with stars in their eyes! Their enthusiasm is palpable.

Specifically... they are eager to encounter the thrill of the Variety Show. "Ooohhhh! I can hardly wait to see what's going to happen!" The Big Game. The Grande Experiment. The Melting Pot. Riding the Rodeo of Life! A Bodacious Opportunity. Create Your Own Adventure. WooHoo! Let's do it!

Some who Incarnate Human on Planet Earth find it disconcerting to live their Life... cheek-to-jowl... with so many others who are deeply ensconced in... weighed down by... ridicule and revenge... fear and misbelief... obstacles and illusions. And, of course, here it is again... the kicker... that deeply ingrained human BIAS... their Belief I Am Separate from God. Separate from Source. (Given even a moment of consideration... how can this possibly *be*?!) This is the unfortunate... unfathomable... misperception which leads to humans being controlled and overpowered by... fear and rage... anxiety and distress... unworthiness and shame. Self-pity.

Naturally... every incarnate human has the ability to choose another evolutionary option. "At their fingertips," as they say. This other option is the choice to be empowered by Love. Compassion. Certainty. Clear vision.

Choices: Overpowered by fear... or... Empowered by Love. Oh, let me think. Um... um. Which shall I choose?! Hmmmm... "I'll take Door #2, Johnny."

As you are busy being Human on Planet Earth... you will be deeply immersed within Love versus Fear. Am I an instrument of Love in this situation? Or am I being an instrument of Fear? The choice is perpetual. Continuous. In every moment.

Speaking of "evolutionary options"... here is a factor seldom pondered before incarnating... but which really must be taken into consideration. Currently, as you are

Human on Planet Earth… you will be working with only about 6% of your conscious creative awareness. 10% tops.

Yes, I know. That does have "major drawback" written all over it. It also offers insight into how it is the human Extra Sensory Faculty is currently set on "mute."

As we consider the 4th Kingdom "brain-mind" capacity… there is so much functionality to reckon with… so much development to accomplish. Shall we dip a toe in?

When it comes to this arena of "brain-mind"… many humans reside in a realm of confusion. They think "brain" and "mind" are the same thing. Which, of course, they are not. Here we have the difference between "hardware" and "software." The brain being the hardware… a tangible organ of the physical body… awash in vast biological chemicals and neurological processes. Certainly impressive. The human brain is the physical organ… the hardware… most frequently associated with mind, consciousness and thinkery.

The human *mind* is the software… the etheric applications… the operating data… and so much more… residing within the invisible.

Mind is the transcendent world of thought and imagination.

Human beings sense this awareness programming within. Nudges. Glimmers. Possibilities. However… simply put… most humans lack their own Aware-O-Meter. They currently have the equipment to touch, express and expand their conscious awareness. They just don't *think* they do.

Consciousness. Realization. Perception. Attitude. Feeling. Belief.

This expansive realm of mind is not confined to the hardware of the brain. The vast, astonishing capacity of mind permeates every cell of the human body. Not just the brain's cells. As the comprehensive presence it is… the mind has extraordinary influence over all body systems.

As we speak here of "conscious creative awareness"… we are speaking of mind… heart… soul… consciousness. Truthfully, human Earthtone language has not yet developed suitable identifying terminology to adequately describe this vast realm of interactive awareness. As mentioned earlier… we speak here of evolutionary processes, particles and elements. The ongoing evolution of human awareness… from the confines of Intellect… to the immense realizations of Intuition and Inspiration.

The human brain… that impressive 3 pound mass of nerve tissue and bio-processes… churns on with all of its Life-sustaining functions. When it comes to the assertion that humans "only use a small percentage of the brain"… some people get testy. "Of course we use all of our brain!" Of course you do. Splitting hairs here.

The aspect humans use only a limited percentage of is the potential of their *mind*. Evidence dwells in the fact… the majority of incarnate humans still reside in the vast, gyrating multi-plex of Intellect. Much ado about all sorts of things. Compete. Contort. Consume.

There are many humans currently living on Planet Earth who are in the early aspirational stages of developing and refining their capabilities within Intuition and Inspiration. These aspirational units are found thru-out the spectrum of human Life… in the cities and urban areas… in the bush, hunting and gathering. Pizza delivery person. Nuclear physicist. Baker. Banker. Boutique owner. An awakening occurs… a developing compulsion… advocating exploration both inner and outer. It doesn't matter where you live or what you do. It matters who you are inside.

I hear what you are thinking… and, yes, you are absolutely right. Residing in diminished mind utilization sets the stage for the great human struggles on Planet Earth: ignorance… greed… anxiety… rage. Poverty… cruelty … harsh judgment… run rampant. And especially burdensome… wallowing in the density of being self-absorbed.

As humans engage more of their awakened mind capacity… they feel no need to grasp and steal… to distort and destroy. It would not occur to them to boast and belittle… to rage and revenge. To take what is not theirs.

These divisive behaviors do not even show up on their radar screen as possible Life choices. Why bother?

Here we have an interesting incarnant fact... utilizing the wealth of increased mind awareness... human understanding naturally evolves to "we're all in this together." Their Life mantra becomes... "How can I best serve others?" Rather than... "Where's more for me?"

Let me be clear in this conversation... it is not my intention to minimize the marvels of the human brain. As you undoubtedly recall... it is the neuroplasticity of this large brain... and its broad operational capacities... that differentiates the Human Kingdom from the Animal.

Animal brains work swell. Their sensory abilities are profound. Sight... smell... hearing... all brain-configured. Animal senses... detecting odors... hearing and interpreting sounds... keen sight... operate way beyond the capability of the same human senses. Animal brains excel at all sorts of unconscious activity. Emphasis on activity... running... leaping... fornicating... foraging... fighting for turf and females.

Where animal awareness is lacking and human awareness excels is that fine and wide arena of being *conscious of self*. Who am I? Where am I? And *being conscious of being conscious*. What am I? Why am I? This makes all the difference.

Think about it. (Ha ha... little joke there.) (Your thinkery *always* wants you to "think about it.")

In humans and vertebrate animals... the brain's mass of nerve tissue is protected by a hard skull. Here in your current B.E. simulator... put your hands on the top of your head. You can feel how hard your skull is. Knock on it. Rock solid.

The skull is a large inverted basket... made of hard bone material. This basket completely covers and protects the brain. It also forms the understructure of your facial plain. Your skull basket, with its various nooks and crannies... sets the distance between your eyes... allowing stereoscopic vision. It determines ear placement to enable sound localization... determining the direction and distance of sounds. Some of these crannies form the sinus cavities... making room for activities that add resonance to your voice... as well as warming and moistening the air which you draw in thru your nostrils.

Your well-protected brain is actually an enlarged extension of your spinal cord. It is the master component of the nervous system. Among other functions... your brain acts as the center of thought. This is the organ that receives and interprets sensory input. It also transmits motor impulses for both gross and fine movement... as well as voluntary and involuntary body processes.

Biologically... in the context of the human body... that brain is one big energy suck. By weight... the brain makes up about 2 percent of the human body. In terms of consuming oxygen and nutrients... that same 2 percent of brain commands up to 20 percent of the body's biological resources. Whoa. No other physical organ devours anything close to that amount.

This grandiose consumption is understandable. The brain itself has a lot going on. It is rife with nerve cells... aka *neurons*... and tissue... "gray matter" and "white matter." This gray matter is actually the outer cortex of nerve cell bodies with their branching dendrites. The white matter is the inner mass of nerve fibers.

There are approximately 100 billion neurons in the human brain. Billion. With a B. As the brain hums along... neurons utilize their dendrites like branches of trees... to transmit along information impulses received from other cells. And yet, as interactive as they are... the branches and neurons never touch each other. Impulses are transmitted via a neurological leap called a synapse. The actual transporting mechanism is a *chemical* messenger... a neurotransmitter.

The work of... the neurons and dendrites... the synapses and neurotransmitters... and the myriad messages they send... are what give humans the ability to think, move, learn, and feel. The complexity of the connections between neurons and the way they travel are key to humans acquiring and utilizing information... realizing... recollecting... furthering brain development.

These synapses... the connecting and communicating leaps between neurons... are the activity... the very foundation... of brain function.

We'll find approximately 1 quadrillion synapses in the human brain. Quadrillion. With a Q. That would be 1,000,000,000,000,000 synapses! There are about a half-billion synapses per cubic millimeter... 0.00006 cubic inch... of brain. Synapses a'plenty. Offering stunning interactive capability.

And that brain is functioning *all* the time. Constantly performing unconscious processes... keeping "the vitals" going... breathing... digesting... regulating heart rate. Eye movement... sound interpretation... hot and cold reflexes... toenail growth.

Cognitive activities also purr along... dreaming... deciding... perceiving... observing... emotionally responding. Choosing.

Human researchers have identified a person's 8 core cognitive capacities. Superb! This not only represents humans pondering and reflecting "outside the box." This moves human awareness of their cognitive capacity *way beyond* the box! Good trans-neurological sleuthing!

As you are about to enter human form... you will find this range of mental options and possibilities quite thrilling! The intellectual inventory researchers have determined offers significant insight into the remarkable human perceptive capabilities. The cognitive skills of developed, mature human mind capacity are recognized as:

Developing the ability to sustain attention… focus… organize mental resources… complete a task.

Being able to restrain abrupt reaction… inhibit reflexive retort… choose a response.

Multiple simultaneous attention… I *love* this one! So useful. Go humans! The current local euphemism = "multi-tasking." (Some folks are better at this than others.) (There are also folks who have opinions as to whether this "context-switching" is truly as efficient and useful as multi-taskers like to think it is.)

Quickly process information… speedy assessments… connections in a blink!

Cognitive flexibility and control… a variation on organizing and directing mental resources. Plasticity. Self-management. A totally useful support mechanism.

Functional memory apparatus… recall and retain capacities… accessing helpful recollections. Value beyond compare.

Recognizing and formulating categories... this fits / that doesn't... distinguishing shared characteristics. This particular element is its own useful convenience.

Comprehending and identifying patterns... compare and contrast... a handy variation on "does this fit?" Configured design. The mosaic of Life unfolding.

Every second, thousands of these incisive cognitive interactions allow the brain to flash-organize myriad memories and stored data into current context. Permitting one to analyze and comprehend... the meaning of a spoken conversation... the content of a written page. To recall a skill to apply in the moment. "Look how this all fits together!"

Rarely are humans aware of their brain's constant, vigilant activity.

Even as the body sleeps, the brain courses with function. Sleep is a fascinating restorative phenomenon. The human instrument fritzes without adequate sleep. The physical, emotional, mental apparatus does not get far without these daily, reinvigorating interludes. When you are human... don't pretend "I don't need much sleep." You do.

Hanging out being Human on Planet Earth is just plain exhausting. Personhooding is an intense, demanding affair. It takes *a lot* of energy. Of all sorts. The human 3-body system sleeps 6–10 hours a day. Literally one third of each 24-hour period is devoted to engaging this Required Essence Stability Technique. You've got to give yourself plenty of R.E.S.T.

The human physical body usually sleeps in a horizontal position... or at times, reclining in a chair. Eyes closed. During sleep, the nervous system becomes relatively inactive. The postural muscles relax. Consciousness is nearly suspended. Of course, the brain continues its various functions... dinner digests... the heart pumps. Inhaling/exhaling. Dreams dreaming. During sleep, the foundational cellular properties of the physical body and the psychological self are set on "cleanse and recharge." This is a very good thing. As I mentioned... an actual Life requirement.

Different areas of brain hardware are working all the time. Yet... as we consider the software... mind... creative conscious awareness... the operational procedures of essence... we find this whole iceberg thing going on. The iceberg is an ideal metaphor for human mind awareness. Generally speaking... conscious activity of the mind = 5 percent... the portion of the awareness iceberg "above the water." Unconscious activity = 95 percent... doing what's doing "below the waterline" of the conscious mind.

In the context of human parlance there is... brain... mind... consciousness.

Not to be confused with the blessing and burden of dormant neural pathways and latent mental ability. Dormant neural stem cells are the source of new neurons in the human brain = the process of neurogenesis. Let us note... this ability to activate new neurons drops with age. The intrinsic mechanisms governing the activating of new neurons declines in the adult human brain. In other planetary systems hosting human units... neurogenesis continues undiminished thru-out a lifetime.

Currently, humans are studying the brain and its myriad functions more effectively than they have been able to in the past. Utilizing highly-developed tools and advanced technologies... researchers have begun to realize ... not just one area of the brain determines cognitive conscious awareness. In the human brain... thinking... formulating... creativity... expression = a collective neural effort.

It's so cool humans are figuring some of this out. Most encouraging. If all continues to go well... this research should lead to welcomed advances in perceptive ability... as well as finer utilization of brain-mind interactivity.

From the human perspective... the great neurological mystery is... how do these diverse regions of the brain collaborate to form conscious experiences? Such a good question! Hey, I'm all for an intriguing mystery.

Did I just hear someone say the Grace of Intuition? Well, uh... yeah. Exactly. The development of Intuition allows incarnate humans to play in a whole different ballpark. The Game evolves.

The evolution of Humankind
resides within their untapped cognitive potential.
Within the untapped areas of mind.

Much of the time with humans of Earth this is the way things stay... untapped. The unfulfilled potential of higher Intellect. Refusing the stretch. Resisting exploration of higher cognitive function. Not responding to that "still, small voice." This is where the inadequate percentage of usage... undeveloped creative mind ability... comes in. Refusing to explore... refusing to trust... the promise of insightful perception. Personal evolution to Intuition... slowed. Sluggish. Untapped.

Yet, all is not befallen to limitation. Built right into the human neural hardware is a fine incarnant gift. Let's give another shout out for *neuroplasticity*! The blessing of developing and extending biological capacity comes sailing thru.

Huzzah!

Chugging along... your ever-capable human brain stands ready. Capable of utilizing all available neural impulses... tissue... synapses. And beyond!

As areas of the brain experience greater neural activity… they consume more oxygen from the blood. Available neural synapses readily recruit that oxygen-rich bio-chemistry into new forms of function. Thus the brain is capable of activating different parts of itself… embracing fresh ideas… learning new skills… developing innovative solutions.

And there you have it! Showing up in the moment. Performing newfound tasks… ideas… perceptions… calculations. Contributing to the ongoing… the onflowing… alchemy of the present.

Show up. Be kind. Contribute. Check. Check. And check.

Brain plasticity on the move! The complex bio-cellular operations of the human brain manufacture new and stronger connections between nerve cells. On the spot! When humans learn… up to 10 billion neurons are making new connections. Zowie! Many times, an individual nerve cell is making hundreds of connections all on its own.

Plasticity = new possibilities! You are equipt! The hardware to support each human's capacity to expand into Intuition and Inspiration is already built in!

As human researchers uncover new brain function indicators, it becomes clear… neuroplasticity is fundamental in the brain's stunning ability to reorganize itself. To change… as it forms new connections between brain cells. This vast realm of potentiality = the basis for human mind software expanding. Upgrading. Moving into, thru-out and beyond Intellect. We are on our way! Embracing the human instrument's next pivotal steps toward Intuition and Inspiration.

Important to note… unless degeneration begins to take place… these expanding possibilities… this ongoing brain regeneration and growth… is available thru-out your entire incarnant Life. Revitalization Rocks!

Bottom line: Human mind capacity for… telepathic ability… extra sensory perception… evolving beyond Intellect to Intuition and Inspiration… is already alive and well within the human wiring framework. These are all human mind capabilities. Built in. If this were not true… how is it some people's lives are graced with these heightened abilities?

Whether it be… karma… dharma… nature… nurture… super-elegant synapses… some humans are able to sense and perceive Life's more refined, ethereal attunements. They use their realizations to be of help… sharing their enhanced discernment… to assist other people in living their lives. Their innate sensitivities reveal what humans are capable of. This is no woo-woo mystery. These "extra-sensory" capabilities reside within each human instrument.

Working in confluence… Life experience completes the brain. Expands the mind. Makes each individual human who they are.

Folks are talented differently. Some incarnate humans remember every detail of every day of their Life... what they wore... what they said... what they ate... who they hung out with. This may seem like some kind of fluke. But, seriously... if *some* people have this degree of Life recall... that would mean the ability to do so is there. Inside *every* human. Untapped.

So here comes a fascinating brain tidbit... this (seemingly) diminished awareness capacity fosters the dynamic for one of the strong attractions... a really big draw... for many who incarnate Human on Planet Earth. It's like a magnetic force. "Come here," it beckons. "Oh yes, come be Human on Planet Earth, my pretty."

Beings are drawn into human form anticipating exactly *this* experience: Absorbed within the mind-numbing bustle of human Life... consciously realizing so little. Then... a glimmer appears. "Could there be more?!" Employing attentive choice and intention... setting in motion the unfolding progression of recall, realization and refinement. "I'm beginning to figure things out!"

To be thick with sleep... then awaken to the rush of fresh potentialities. Whoa. Good stuff.

This unfolding comes your way thru humankind's signature modality... that ever-reliable... tho at times frustrating... hit-or-miss process. Hints and clues. Breadcrumbs. Could it be?! Waiting for someone else to "tell me." Realizing... it is mine to figure out. To release to. To embrace. On my own.

This rush of potential conscious conceptualizing has huge appeal. You'll find it goes something like this: Here I be, rattling around in the agitated fog of being human... when... Jumpin' Jehoshaphat! Is *that* the spark of awakened awareness awakening!? It *is*!

I am all over nourishing that spark! I choose and persevere. I exercise my awareness. My awakeness. My perseverance *does* further. I experience living this human Life from a different perspective! I see the bliss of being here in human form! I embody my true purpose. I now *know* I am Spirit living a human experience.

Zowie! This is one delectable rush! ("How can I *be* so lucky!?")

Becoming more aware... actualized... functional. The thrill of it!

Remembering your Whole Self. Whole. Not just a bunch of individuated parts grasping at the concept... the possibility of Wholeness. Filling the gaps with conscious awareness. The whole enchilada. With cheese.

There *you* are... in the thick of this ongoing unfolding. This miraculous adventure. Clarification. Sparkles! Innovation. Brilliance! Moving from density to radiance... all while ensconced in human form. Gives me thrill bumps just talking about it!

This is what draws so many to incarnate as Earthtone humans… "I'm finding my way thru density and delusion to greater realization!" The serene beauty of the lotus blossoming from its mud-bound roots. Harmony thru conflict. Releasing and repurposing calcified Life energy. Grace unshackled from grudgement. Once again embracing The Truth of Life. The Light is *real*. All this realizing… actualizing… as I am still incarnate in human form. Indescribably delicious.

Great strides are currently being made in this very direction.

As we speak… the Khalifs of Intuition are bathing the neurons of every incarnant human with higher frequencies of Light Certainty. These frequencies are more refined than conscious awareness has ever experienced… since first beginning to embody in physical Earthtone reality, eons ago.

Biologically… this more elaborate dose of Intuitive Awareness In Action is Lighting Up! each human being's higher frequency glands… pituitary, pineal, and hypothalamus.

This activity introduces excitation to the ganglionic centers at the base of the brain. Each gland and ganglion is lifted… infused with Light… allowing the awakened bliss of full functioning awareness.

Your human awakening continues to unfold. Life looks different. Life feels different. Because you are different… inside. Never to be the same again.

All this is taking place in the confluence... the very midst... of the engaging phenomena of that ever-captivating HazMat Variety Show. There's lots to do... amusing and otherwise... when you are busy being Human on Planet Earth. Plenty of variety. Plenty of hazardous materials. Plenty of show.

Another supreme attraction as you take human form on Planet Earth = the vast and varied incarnant locales. For a not-very-large planet... with so much of its surface covered in water... it's right impressive how many different venues Earth's humans have to choose from.

Currently, the most significant difference in locale you'll notice since your last incarnation, will be the many gigantic urban centers bustling on every continent. Stuffed with people and activity... traffic and concrete... cacophonous din and cultural festivities. Living in a big city offers a vast and varied range of experiences... in childhood and thru-out adult Life. Neither better nor worse... but certainly very different... than the Life content available in rural and isolated locales inhabited by only a few.

Urban and congested vs. rural and isolated = the 2 poles of potential locale. Vast venue variations exist between these 2 poles of possibility. Small towns. A thriving metropolis. Tribal villages. Island Life. University towns. Ranches and farms. Kibbutz and commune. Each instilled with its own opportunities and drawbacks. Every locale offering diverse Life development issues and transactions.

As an incarnant... your thoughts, beliefs, and attitudes... about yourself... about others... about Life... will be completely informed and colored by where you grow up. On the savanna. In the mountains. Near an ocean. In the desert. In a penthouse. On a tropical island. Surrounded by big trees. Where there are no trees. In a tenement or barrio. In the treetops. On a sampan or a sailboat. Out where the deer and the antelope play.

Again, let me say... great swaths of the planet's surface are covered by water. Remarkably... 70% of the globe is covered by ocean... holding 96.5% of all of Earth's water. Add to that... lakes and rivers... wetlands and swamps... ponds and streams... vast accumulations of frozen ice. That's a *lot* of H_2O. Did you catch how I did that? I tossed in a Planet Earth science moniker. H_2O is the chemical symbol used by many humans to denote water. This represents 2 hydrogen atoms (H_2) bonded to 1 oxygen atom (O) = the configuration forming 1 molecule of water. I'm sure you've noticed... many times on Planet Earth, there is more than 1 way to say the same thing.

I know some of you find this frustrating... but, again I will mention... the human instrument, with its current set of accessories... is not equipt to breathe underwater. I know... it does seem an odd physical limitation, considering The Gods of Hydration have blessed Earth with so much wondrous water. But there you have it. During the time period you will soon be incarnate... there will be no choosing to take form as mermaid nor merman. Not gonna happen.

Yes... there is breathing equipment you can wear for brief, submerged excursions. As we did earlier with the help of Realizmotron... swimming with dolphins. But do not anticipate enjoying languid interludes in mystical underwater caves. There will be no extended frolicking with delightful sea creatures. Not this time.

Along a related line... according to locale... it is possible for a person to live an entire incarnation without ever seeing an ocean. In some cases, without even *knowing* such phenomenal *aqua firma* exists on Planet Earth. This is astounding to me. Can you even *imagine*?! As one who finds great pleasure interacting with the ocean... swimming in it... kayaking on it... doing Tai Chi with it... sitting and looking at it... it's hard to imagine living an entire human Life without ever seeing it. Without even knowing about it. But such are the variants on Planet Earth.

In human time demarcation... you will be incarnating during the latter half of the 20th Century and thru-out the 21st. More than likely, you have had previous Earthtone incarnations in which you have experienced... the slower pace... the dusty distances... the rhythm of Life... as it has played out on Planet Earth for countless centuries. That "rhythm" has changed. Especially in urban and sub-urban areas... things have way speeded up.

You will be amazed how connected most every place is these days... by roads and highways... airplanes and shipping... telephones... television... internet. It's a whole different ballgame. Safe to say, currently on Planet Earth... in the majority of Life arenas... in most ways and means... this sure ain't your Grandpappy's ballgame.

Over the course of untold centuries... humankind on Earth developed in isolated pockets. Incubating. Naturally, this led to the expression of vastly different... cultures... cuisine... education... music... dance… architecture. Each of these areas developed its own language and way of speaking. As you incarnate on Planet Earth this time, there will be more than 2,000 spoken languages. When you consider... dialects... pidgin... patois... idioms... this number rises even higher. Easy to see how confusion runs rampant. "What'd she say!?"

Almost all of Earth's current languages have a written as well as a spoken form. Complete alphabets. Rules of pronunciation. Grammar usage.

Adding to the linguistic confusion... with so many different word-sounds for the human ear to hear... in some languages... one word-sound can be used to describe completely different items or states. For example, in the language English... the word-sound "plane" (pronounced *playn*) can mean both... a sharp tool a woodworker uses to create a join or smooth a surface... or a vessel which flies thru the air carrying freight, mail, and passengers. Alter the spelling just a bit to "plain"... the same word-sound can now mean... a broad, open expanse of land... an item, simple and unadorned... or a detail, evident and obvious. That's just plain true.

Don't even get me started on to, two and too. Or there, their, and they're.

This multitude of Earthtone word-sounds and languages is a prime motivating factor for the advent of the word "Maylaigh." As you undoubtedly recall, this new, inspired word has been circulating on Planet Earth for the last few decades. The word Maylaigh means "The Love That Heals." Specifically, *that* word means specifically *that* Love.

To move beyond this Earthtone complication of so many differing languages and parlance... the intention of delivering the word-sound Maylaigh into the human ear and vocabulary... allows an opportunity for clarity and inclusion. As a Spaniard says "Maylaigh" to a Ugandan... even tho they are not able to effectively communicate in each other's language... they *will* both know what that word means. They will both know they speak of The Love That Heals.

The dissemination and use of the word Maylaigh is recognized as a tangible step in the evolution of human awareness. A conscious step toward embracing and developing the Truth of Healing Love in human hearts and minds. Definitely in human interactions.

This evolvement reveals Humankind's unfolding progress toward embracing and developing that treasure of human birthright... Intuition and Inspiration.

As a longtime observer of Life on Planet Earth... I find the development of human communication quite intriguing. Speaking. Writing. Counting. Texting.

You may recall... much of the initial movement and emergent communication between Earth's far-flung areas was motivated by the trading of goods: my fish for your cinnamon... your animal hides for my dried corn... your amber for my fine silk cloth.

In order to measure or weigh items... to count and quantify goods exchanged... humans developed symbols depicting numbers. Along with numbers came systems of accounting and inventory. Numbers were widely used many centuries before the formulation of letters to signify word sounds. This, of course, led to the transcription of language and spoken intent. Scrolls. Manuscripts. Documents. Books.

Their compulsion to trade goods motivated humans to design and build water traveling vessels. These water craft proceeded to locomote trade far and beyond. Over time... humans evolved their canoes and boats into ships for marine warfare. Larger boats allowed for delivering numbers of people... gear... armaments... horses... to the shores of islands and continents where, otherwise, these invaders... these marauders and conquerors... would have never been able to set foot.

As is the human way... the invaders believed they were far superior and their ways were always right and best. The *only* way! The indigenous were seen merely as ignorant heathens. Rather than attempting to understand the locals and learn to appreciate their ways... these invaders believed it was their "right" to "own" this new land and dominate the folks who already lived there. War. Conquer. Victory! I've got a flag!

"I plant the flag! In the name of the Queen." The King. Whomever. Basically saying... "Mine!" "All this land and these resources are now mine." Or the Queen's. Or somebody's. "This all certainly is not yours any more, you illiterate savage." The conquerors' belief in their own vast superiority permits them to see the original inhabitants as mere pagan. Viewing those conquered... as diminished... less than human. Slaves.

Conquering foreign shores is one aspect of intentional human upheaval. War is another. I am at a loss here. What to even say about Earth's humans as they continue to insist upon demonstrating their war-making ways? As part of your Orientation... I am supposed to speak with you about humans and their addiction to war. I notice I've been putting it off.

Evidently, Earthtone humans cannot figure out how to interact without warring. Without atrocities. Without cruelty. The 2 "World Wars" tore the heart out of the 20th century. Only to be followed by more wars. And assassinations. More violence. More lives completely up-ended.

Make note for your Earthing Now Multiple Choice Exam. You'll come across these 3 questions:

1. Where does humankind demonstrate its inability to negotiate... to articulate intelligently... and craft viable, non-violent solutions? The answer is war.
2. What is the clearest example of humans losing their way in a wasteland of useless upheaval as they continue their efforts to develop Intellect beyond Instinct? Again, the answer is the human propensity for war.
3. What appears to be humanity's favored population control device? War.

The HazMat Variety Show

Those who decry The HazMat Variety Show are quick to point to Earthlings' ongoing hostility and aggression as prime evidence of the rather hopeless... less than evolving... state of affairs on Planet Earth. The skeptics readily remark, "Earth humans are not even able to effectively negotiate their differences." This is condemned by many as a pathetic plight. A pathetic blight. Observed with more than a little snark. Truth is... humans *can* come together. They *can* collaborate... and actually craft solutions. I've seen it... been part of it. Those who snark are, understandably, impatient. Frustrated. You may recall mention of humanity's misuse of the snail's pace clause. These skeptics are also showing their inclination to focus on the worst when it suits them... not unlike certain incarnate humans.

Instead of calmly discussing differences and evenly finding solutions... Earthtone humans' first inclination = resorting to... yelling... insulting... name-calling. Watch... this quickly escalates to... bashing... exploding... pillaging. Serious impulse-control issues. The tribulations of wildly coursing testosterone. Unchecked.

Old men... in the grip of... aroused by... the sorcery of their own ego-driven captivations. Or their shameful mistakes. Reminiscent of male elephant seals crashing and bashing against each other when they are in heat. These male humans... these aged alpha dogs... in an effort to mark and claim their territory... to make sure they get their point across... send younglings off to fight for them. (How many old men do you see on the battlefield? Not many.) "You must advance my power!" "You must defend the Motherland!" "Get me more territory!" "Off to war, you young pups!" Cannon fodder.

Another war. Senseless feuding. Each generation has its war(s). Cutting down young men and women before they even have time to live. A new generation... each incarnant moving toward a rich and rewarding Life... sucked into and destroyed by appalling conflict. The heart of possibility devastated. Such desolation. Such waste.

War and ongoing aggression = an active, distractive issue on Planet Earth. As you are human, it won't take you long to detect conflict and its sidekick, combat. You may be born into a military family... or even into a "war zone." Your entire childhood may be circumscribed by the trauma of death and destruction. Difficulty and disaster. The sounds of explosions and gunfire might be the audio backdrop of your youngling Life.

As if human Life is not complicated... "hard enough"... already. There you are... an innocent bystander... toiling to survive... doing all you can... feeding your family... managing Life's responsibilities. Then, war is upon you. Thru no fault of your own... except being the wrong color or in the wrong place or of the wrong tribe. War. Exploding. Destruction comes to you. Consumes your Life. Hundreds of thousands of human lives are upended by the atrocities of war every year. Barbaric. Cruel. Unnecessary.

War is pointless. It never ends.

War and the vicious brutality of violence… delivers us to an astute human observation: "Violence is the last refuge of the incompetent."

As noted previously… humans continue to burn fossil fuels. Mining. Drilling. Igniting long-buried plant matter and decomposed animal biology from countless centuries past. To heat their homes and energize their manufacturing. Tons of pollutants released… fouling the air… lifting into the atmosphere. Making toxic the water. As well as the soil.

Humans are stunningly good at fouling their nest.

What can they possibly be thinking?

Does thinking even come into it?

Humans express disgust at rats fouling their nests. Really? Humans rollick right along… fouling every one of their Life-support systems.

Earth's humans have the smarts… and the resources… to devise other energy-generating technologies.

We have already mentioned the current obstacle… greed. Malfeasance. Those who covet their financial profits scurry to convince others, "The profound mess being made here does not 'really' matter." Convincing, short-sighted persuasion. Many of their fellow humans choose to believe them and turn a blind eye.

Have you heard of "fracking?" Unbelievable. Destruction and pollution of valuable resources. Beyond short-sighted. Very big damage for very little "profit." Oh, those humans… and their "bottom line."

Constant war… plundering resources… polluting water, air, and soil. Lives lost. Not all dead. Just lost.

Stupefying mismanagement.

Really. What *are* Earth's current humans thinking? Certainly not about what condition they are leaving the planet in. Nor about the well-being of the generations to follow. Limited awareness brings limited… self-serving… results.

"Don't even bother me about my impact on 'others'."

"Who cares about 'them'?"

"This is all about me. And more stuff… for me."

"I really don't care. Do you?"

I'll tell you what… it's annoying talking about human war and greed and blatant short-sightedness. Let's move on from that storm of stupidity. You'll be up to your elbows in it soon enough.

Have you heard about Earth's weather? Climate. Atmospheric conditions. Weather is certainly a locales-related phenomenon. It could factor into your considerations about where you'll live out your upcoming incarnation. On Planet Earth... you've got it all... dry and cold... hot and steamy. And every imaginable actuality in between.

There's even a dot of land in the middle of Earth's vast Pacific Ocean... an island called Hawaii... where you can surf in the morning and ski in the afternoon. In fact, nearly all of Earth's diverse climate zones are found on this one particular, isolated spot of land.

In our earlier discussions about different aspects of Life on Earth... we've talked about various poles and spectra within the realms of human endeavor. The planet itself even comes with 2 poles. And definitely with the spectra of everything in between. On Planet Earth, the poles reside at the top and the bottom of the planet. Each has a name. *Arctic* is the North Pole... currently at the top of the planet. *Antarctic* is the name given to the South Pole... at the bottom of the planet.

Vast areas of each pole are perpetually covered in ice and snow. Due to their positions on the planetary sphere... the angle of the sun is horizontal as it hits these polar regions. This has its effect on both temperature and the amount of light and dark. When you live near the poles... you live in 6 months of daylight... and 6 months of darkness. Even during the 6 months of daylight... it's still right chilly at these far reaches. During the 6 months of dark... it's *really* cold. As a human, if you were there... you'd be bundled up. Wearing many layers of skins and clothing. Just to stay reasonably warm and able to function.

Here's an interesting distinction between Earth's 2 poles... the Arctic, surrounding the North Pole, is a frozen ocean. Antarctica... which surrounds the South Pole... is a frozen continent. It's the 5th largest continent... larger than all of Europe. The oceans around each Pole are rich in nutrients and abundant with sea Life.

You won't find a lot of humans living close to these poles. As the largest "cold desert" on the planet, Antarctica is an environment inhospitable to Life... except if you be a penguin or a seal. Or bacteria or algae. Or mites. The Antarctic region has no permanent human population.

Interestingly... as many as 30 different countries operate scientific research stations on Antarctica. Some are there only in the summer. Some are there year-round. The latter is hard to even imagine = all snow all the time. And extraordinarily fierce winds... whipping near constantly. Snow and blow.

During the summer season, around 4,000 people support and perform scientific projects on the frozen continent and nearby islands. This number drops to approximately 1,000 researchers during the winter. In addition to these permanent, year-round research stations... during the summer season there can be about 30 field camps thru-out the Antarctic region for people conducting scientific projects.

If the Antarctic intrigues you... you will have to go there as an adult. You won't be a kid growing up there. You'll want to educate yourself... acquire an advanced degree or 3 in fields of scientific endeavor. Or learn to cook or fix things and offer support services. You can get yourself there. You've just really got to want to.

On literally the other side of the planet... the Inuit, indigenous human populations, do inhabit areas of the Arctic. The vexatious elements make sure they work hard to survive there. The harsh Arctic environment makes it difficult for people to grow their own food. Historically, these peoples have been disinclined to even give that a try. They do, however... collect... eat... and store... the various roots, stems and berries (I've heard they're delicious) of plants growing in their vicinity during the short summer months.

By necessity, mainly carnivorous... the diet of these Arctic indigenous folks consists of a variety of fish, seal, whale, and caribou. Different Inuit groups favor reindeer meat or walrus. For some, bear really hits the spot. Not only do they eat the flesh and muscle of these animals... they also consume their blood, blubber, and vitamin-rich internal organs. No good reason to be choosy while eking out survival in such an unforgiving environment.

Nothing goes to waste. The animal bones, fur, skin, and sinew have long been used to make boots, clothing, and mittens. To craft tools. To make drums, masks, and carvings for rituals and dancing. Bird skins and feathers are used for their charm and decoration.

Polar bear and seal skins prove to be naturally waterproof. Oil from the fat of seals, whales, and other marine mammals is the primary source of fuel for lamps and to heat dwellings. And here's a clever one... fish skin attached to the soles of shoes. The fish scales provide good traction on the slippery ice and snow.

Talk about making good use of every thing... a traditional article of Arctic clothing... the parka... is frequently made from *gut skin*. That is gut, as in intestines. It turns out mammal intestines... cleaned, dried and sewn together... make a parka that is both lightweight and water repellent. Who knew? This particular, very useful parka covers fur clothing... which would otherwise be ruined... while climbing around inside a whale carcass to butcher meat. My hat is off to the folks who figured out how to make durable, mess-resistant clothing out of mammal guts! Kudos.

Worthy to note... you *can* be born into an Arctic indigenous family and spend your childhood... perhaps your entire incarnation... living in that cold and captivating region. It would have its perks. You be thinking warm thoughts now.

On the other hand... a useful human colloquialism indicating, "here's an opposite factor"... if you were to draw a line around the widest part of Earth's sphere... there you'd have what is referred to as the Equator. Whereas, at the poles, the angle of the sun at noon is horizontal... at the Equator, the angle of the sun at noon is perpendicular. Straight up. Or shining straight down, as the case may be. This leads to 2 engaging factors affecting living Life near the Equator:

1. Days and nights... light and dark... are nearly equal amounts of time. All year long.
2. With sunlight beaming at the Earth around the Equator more strongly than at the poles... it is warm there. Really warm. And humid. Muggy. Sultry. All year long.

Clothes... ha! Why bother?! Except for protecting your skin wrapper from the incessant sun... forget about those extra layers. The fewer bits of clothing you have on... the better.

We had an excellent example of this climate zone's hot and humid in our earlier Orientation Moment, when Realizmotron took us on a tour of Amazonia... the Rain Forest. Lush, for sure. Definitely residing in the realm of hot and sweaty.

Now let's give our attention to the weather between the polar regions and the equator. The majority of land masses on Planet Earth lie between these 2 points of extreme. Here in the "between," we find... Ta Da!... The *Seasons*. Spring. Summer. Autumn. Winter. The cycle of Life... blossoms... growth... fall... cold. All foretold by the ebb and flow of light. Longer days and shorter nights gleefully speak of summer. Shorter days and longer nights mark the chill of winter.

You may recall these seasonal cycles from past incarnations. Life awakens in the spring... seeds are planted. With increasing light as the days grow longer... crops flourish thru the summer. Chilled beverages are consumed. Circulating fans are engaged to stir the warm air. In autumn... the grown crops are harvested. Canned, dried, stored. The days are getting shorter... there is less light. Leaves fall... temperatures begin to cool. Winter leads to hibernation... scraping ice from windshields... festivities to brighten spirits. Let's sip warm beverages while we stay indoors out of the cold! Got any board games we can play? Charades, anyone?

Climate offers fascinating variations on living the day-to-day. Footwear fashionistas pull on their stylish boots in winter... and bring out their strappy sandals in summer. There are variations within the variations. Generally... flowers bloom in the spring... crops grow during the warm summer days. Unless you happen to live in monsoon regions... where this spring/summer cycle shows up as rain. Rain. And. Rain. In many areas, winter brings snow. But not everywhere.

In the snowy climes, humans have devised numerous ways to amuse themselves... sledding... ice skating... snowboarding... skiing... both down the hills and across the country. And there's always ice fishing... sitting in a tiny hut on a frozen lake... around a hole cut in the ice. Watching your fishing line. Freezing your patooties off. Some people do this every year. They'll tell you they actually like it. Oh... in this case... "your patooties" references your bottom... your derriere... your bum. Probably, in the case of ice fishing... your whole body... not just your patootie... will become most seriously chilled.

So many possible places to live out your incarnation... so many languages, fashions, and foods. So many climate factors to learn to thrive in. Adding to the mix... different people in different places have different priorities... different customs. Different beliefs about Life. Different ways of interacting. This can, at times, present a clash, as people in these modern times move from one cultural venue to another.

In the long ago on Planet Earth, folks lived their Life... grew to adulthood, reproduced and died... in the same locale where they were born. Now... in this current "busy, busy" fast-paced epoch... many people move from place to place... by choice. Some, by necessity. Moving from locale to locale is much more of an option than it once was. "Let's go check out a different venue!" Sometimes it is a requirement. "We have out-fished the local area." "My job transferred me to another city."

There are times when moving to a new venue includes learning to communicate in a new language. Many people learn to speak more than only the language of their birth locale. This is called being multilingual. In this current epoch... speaking more than one language can be a real boon to navigating human Life. Making friends and connexions... ordering at restaurants...finding your way around.

Moving about the planet... or even in the same city... is certainly an educational experience. Including also much potential to be mind-expanding.

Now that you've heard about some of your venue choices... and climate components... you are welcome to visit our Interpretorium Locales Library. There, your Bio Energy simulator is able to engage Realizmotron dioramas to actually move around in and explore many of the different possibilities and scenarios.

For your amusement... choose a particular locale, and you can adjust Realizmo's whiz knobs to go back and forward in time in that venue. For fun. Observing times and events... not interacting.

This "time travel" is not something you'll be able to do while incarnate human. Not yet. As with shape-shifting, breathing underwater, and extra sensory perception… time travel is not currently on the list of incarnant options. But you'll have fun in the Realizmotron dioramas. They're quite engaging. Certainly informative.

Before you affix your moniker to your final Human Incarnant release form… you will be asked to choose your 5 top destination selections. Of course, I'd like to tell you you'll get your first choice. That happens sometimes. But, not always. There are karmic components… considerations… consequences… weaving thru the fabric of Your Etheric Sconce which will determine your actual birth destination and childhood environment.

We do want to know where you'd like to show up on Planet Earth. But, no guarantees. As you can imagine… it's complicated.

To be asked where you would like to show up is a hallmark of this particular Orientation Pod. Such interest in your locale choice is not a regular feature in most pre-incarnant pods. The majority of incarnating humans are not given choice. As a result of those aforementioned considerations and karmic components… most incarnants get plopped down where they can best pick up the thread to work with current versions of past-Life factors and future associations.

Now... speaking of complicated. Ha! We are going to segue into the realm of human relationship communication. Look out!

During our first Orientation Moment... you may recall, I mentioned 3 items of human perception: Interpretation. Communication. Miscommunication.

1. **Interpretation**: Why is this called *The Interpretorium*? Because as you are human... your *interpretations* weave the fabric of your Life... rendering the texture of your beliefs. About yourself. About others. About Life. As you interpret... each and every thing... so do you believe. Your interpretations are the bedrock of your personal truth. Your story. Your "version" of what is happening to you. Which becomes exactly what *is* happening to you. Gross or groovy.

2. **Communication**: Human communication is often a rather cumbersome process. Your ears hearing... or your eyes reading... ignites your brain neurons to roam thru your internal compilation of attitudes and experience filters. Your brain translates words and experiences into concepts and information. Your neural receptors... traveling thru these various incarnant and karmic interpretive filters... are

stimulated to process input. This multi-layered activity generates your perception of what is being conveyed. Which then determines your output.

3. **Miscommunication**: As you output... you may experience unexpected and inexplicable communication outcomes. What you are saying... or what you intend... can easily not be heard nor experienced by the other person as what you meant. This is because what you are attempting to communicate travels thru the other person's filters and attitudes... their compilation activity. Yes... this can lead to unintentional blunders... gaffes... misunderstandings... even conflict. Times like this... human communication can be clunky. Poorly nuanced. Frustrating.

On Planet Earth... as within every human-based zone... communication... understanding... especially relationship... are significant Life factors. *Muy importante*. Truthfully, these are the factors that can "make it" or "break it" as you are tootling around being human.

As I just mentioned... what is intended by one person is not always what the other person interprets or experiences. Miscommunication is not just one person's "fault." It takes 2 to tango. To give you a whiff of a clue as to how human "mis-understanding" can play out... we are going to again engage the wonders of Realizmotron... to create humanesque scenarios for your observation.

These scenarios employ the ever-popular boy-meets-girl motif... that attention-grabbing dynamic which enchants and engrosses a great deal of human energy. These very interactions are often rife with misinterpretation.

Our scenario will be a "blind date." A blind date is when friends of 2 people say to each of them... "I know somebody you should meet." It used to be that the "introducing person" would set a time and place for them to meet each other. Now, in these "modern times"... with an exchange of contact information... phone numbers or email addys... the 2 people set up the date for themselves. Bottom line: The 2 people are meeting each other for the first time as they arrive for their agreed-upon date.

We offer this scenario today for you to observe... the way(s) different people react differently to exactly the same communication situation.

Let me conclude my preface by saying, as I have before... when communication between humans does work... 'tis a lovely thing. Despite an array of obstacle illusions... humans do manage to connect. Harmony prevails. The outcome of skillful, attuned communication is well-worth the effort.

Much of the time, there is definitely plenty of effort involved.

Now... sit back... relax. As I fire-up Realizmotron... these interactions will be playing out right in front of us, here. Oh... I should've brought popcorn. Ah, well. Our set-up... the premise... of each scenario will be exactly the same. Observe the reactions and responses of the person who opens the door. And the effect they have in the world of our young man.

And we begin:

A good-looking young man, Mick, is walking up to a house. He is here to meet Cass, a young woman he does not know. On their blind date... they plan to go to dinner. As he drove here... the rear tire on his car blew. He had to stop to fix it. He is close to an hour late. Due to his cell phone battery being dead... he has not taken the time to call her.

Mick is thinking: *Took me long enough to find a place to park. Shoot... I hope my shirt doesn't stink. It's so hot. I don't want to look like a total sweat-jerk when she opens the door. I can't believe I'm so late.* Mick walks up to the front porch. *Nice place.* Lifting his hand to knock on the front door... *Oh Geez. What was I thinking saying yes to a blind date!*

Before Mick can even knock... the door flies open.

"You are too late! Jerk! I've been sitting here for more than an hour being stood-up! You could have called! How dare you even show your face!! You've totally ruined my evening. Get out of here before I call the police, you low-life." She slams the door shut.

Mick stands there, stunned. *Shit. I knew I should have called her when I got that flat. I should have looked for a phone. I should've had my phone battery charged. I should've... I was in a rush. I had to fix that stupid flat. I got here as fast as I could. I should have let her know. Shit. Now what am I going to do with this retro orchid wrist corsage I brought her? Somebody would like it. Aunt Mil would... but I'm sure not giving it to her. She'd never believe I had gotten it just for her. She'd want to know the whole story. Not gonna go there.*

Jake's Cantina is near here. I'll just drive on over and see what's going on there. Glad I found out Cass is such a bitch right up front. She didn't even give me a chance to explain. Or even open my mouth! If I had a minute, I could've told her what happened. She didn't even give me a chance to get a word in. I'm glad I don't have to go on a date with her.

Reboot...

A good-looking young man, Mick, is walking up to a house. He is here to meet Cass, a young woman he does not know. On their blind date... they plan to go to dinner. As he drove here... the rear tire on his car blew. He had to stop to fix it. He is close to an hour late. Due to his cell phone battery being dead... he has not taken the time to call her.

Mick is thinking: *Took me long enough to find a place to park. Shoot... I hope my shirt doesn't stink. It's so hot. I don't want to look like a total sweat-jerk when she opens the door. I can't believe I'm so late.* Mick walks up to the front porch. *Nice place.* Lifting his hand to knock on the front door... *Oh Geez. What was I thinking saying yes to a blind date!*

Mick knocks 3 different times before Cass opens the door. She's wearing a pink camisole top and jeans... the long-stemmed glass in her hand has a smidge of white wine in the bottom. She lights up as she sees Mick. "Oh my God! You are as good looking as Janie said you were! Come on in. Do you want a glass of wine? I only have white. Tonight, Sauvignon Blanc. I don't drink red wine. It does a number on my stomach. I might have a beer in the fridge. Or there's a bottle of Jameson's. What's your pleasure?"

Whoa! What a hottie! This is looking real good already! "Hey, I'm happy to drink Sauvignon Blanc."

"Great! Come on back to the kitchen with me. It's so hot. You don't mind I'm in just my cami, do you? I took my blouse off half an hour ago. When it's this hot, I usually just walk around the house naked."

"Hey, sorry I'm late. I had a flat tire."

Looking back over her shoulder with a smile, Cass says, "That's okay. I figured something came up. No worries. I'm good at entertaining myself."

Wow. What a stellar chick!

"I know a really cool place to go for dinner. Moroccan food. We can walk there from here. Most guys I know like beer or whiskey. You sure you want white wine?"

"Works for me. I have good friends who drink white wine. I like the buzz."

"Alright then. Here's your glass. I find that 'only serving 1/3 of a glass of wine' shit annoying. Sometimes restaurants don't even pour to 1/3. I always like to fill the glass full."

"Thanks. In Hawaii, they say Mahalo."

"I *love* Hawaii!! My Aunt Mil lives in Kona! I've visited her every year since I was a kid!"

"You have an Aunt Mil?!"

"Yeah, Milly Sue Gallagher. She hates Milly Sue. So unless we want to bug her, we call her Mil."

"No way! *I* have an Aunt Mil."

"Get out of here!"

"Here name is Millicent. She hates her name, too. It so doesn't fit her. I've always known her as Aunt Mil. She really bristles when someone calls her Millicent... like it's an insult."

"That is so trippy! How many people have an Aunt Mil?! Lots of Aunt Sues or Aunt Cathys, even Aunt Brittany... but Aunt Mil?! I've never met anyone else with an Aunt Mil."

"She's my favorite aunt."

"My Aunt Mil is my favorite aunt, too! You know, another Hawaiian tradition is to take your shoes off when you come inside. Go ahead... kick off your shoes. We don't have to leave for the restaurant right away. Get comfy. The breeze from the ceiling fans has cooled things off some. Just getting the air circulating really helps. Here, let me top off your glass. I've got a head start on you."

"Hey... I brought you this retro orchid wrist corsage."

"Shut up! That is so cool! I love the color. Nobody's *ever* given me a wrist corsage before. Ha ha... how very dapper, indeed."

Reboot ...

A good-looking young man, Mick, is walking up to a house. He is here to meet Cass, a young woman he does not know. On their blind date... they plan to go to dinner. As he drove here... the rear tire on his car blew. He had to stop to fix it. He is close to an hour late. Due to his cell phone battery being dead... he has not taken the time to call her.

Mick is thinking: *Took me long enough to find a place to park. Shoot... I hope my shirt doesn't stink. It's so hot. I don't want to look like a total sweat-jerk when she opens the door. I can't believe I'm so late.* Mick walks up to the front porch. *Nice place.* Lifting his hand to knock on the front door... *Oh Geez. What was I thinking saying yes to a blind date!*

Mick knocks on the door several times. As he waits, he starts thinking... *Looks like nobody's home. I don't see any lights on. Wait. Is that someone walking around in there. Did the curtain just move? Is someone crying? What the...?*

A piece of paper slips out from under the front door... "Go away."

Ah Geez... Now what am I going to do with this retro orchid wrist corsage I brought her? I knew this date wasn't a good idea.

Reboot...

A good-looking young man, Mick, is walking up to a house. He is here to meet Cass, a young woman he does not know. On their blind date... they plan to go to dinner. As he drove here... the rear tire on his car blew. He had to stop to fix it. He is close to an hour late. Due to his cell phone battery being dead... he has not taken the time to call her.

Mick is thinking: *Took me long enough to find a place to park. Shoot... I hope my shirt doesn't stink. It's so hot. I don't want to look like a total sweat-jerk when she opens the door. I can't believe I'm so late.* Mick walks up to the front porch. *Nice place.* Lifting his hand to knock on the front door... *Oh Geez. What was I thinking saying yes to a blind date!*

After a couple of knocks... Cass opens the door. Mick blurts out, "I'm sorry I'm so late. I know I should have called you. I'm Mick. I had a flat tire. It blew my mind. I just wanted to get the tire changed and get here. I'm sorry I didn't call. Here, I've got an orchid wrist corsage for you. It's retro. I liked it when I saw it at the flower shop. Thought you might like it, too."

"Whoa. Steady, big fella. Hi Mick. I'm Cass. No worries. Nice to meet you. Step into the air conditioning. Looks like you could use a cold drink. Coke? Ice tea? A beer? I'm all for hydration. Follow me to the kitchen. Thanks for the wrist corsage. It's cool. Orchids are my favorite flower. Great color! I'll wear it to dinner.

"I'm immersed in this sculpture I've been working on. I decided not to change my clothes until after you got here. Open the fridge and get yourself something to drink. Ice in the freezer. I'm heading back to my studio. It's back this way. You'll be able to find it after you've gotten your drink. I've been sipping a glass of Maker's on the rocks. The bottle's on the counter, if you'd like that. Bring whatever you're drinking back here. I have a little more work I want to do on this piece. We can talk about where we want to go eat."

Mick thinks to himself... *Wow. She's fascinating. And what a cool place. I like artistic women. This could work out.*

Reboot...

A good-looking young man, Mick, is walking up to a house. He is here to meet Cass, a young woman he does not know. On their blind date... they plan to go to dinner. As he drove here... the rear tire on his car blew. He had to stop to fix it. He is close to an hour late. Due to his cell phone battery being dead... he has not taken the time to call her.

Mick is thinking: *Took me long enough to find a place to park. Shoot... I hope my shirt doesn't stink. It's so hot. I don't want to look like a total sweat-jerk when she opens the door. I can't believe I'm so late.* Mick walks up to the front porch. *Nice place.* Lifting his hand to knock on the front door... *Oh Geez. What was I thinking saying yes to a blind date!*

One knock. The door flies open. A big, burly guy... well over 6 feet tall... and broad... is standing there. He doesn't look happy. "Hey, pretty boy," he says. "I'm Cassie's big brother, Jake. What makes you think you can treat my sister this way? You said you were going to be here over an hour ago. What's the deal, man?"

"Uh... oh... uh... I got a flat tire. My cell phone was dead. I changed the tire as fast as I could. Then when I got here, I couldn't find a place to park. I didn't mean to be so late."

"Yeah... you say. Wait a minute." Jake bangs the door shut.

Oh shit. This is ridiculous. I'm sweating like a pig. Do pigs really sweat? I am never going on a blind date again... ever. This sucks.

Several minutes go by. Jake opens the door again. "There's a vegetarian cafe across the street... 2 blocks that way. Look for some colored banners. Cass says she'll meet you there in 15 minutes. She'll have a red hibiscus in her hair. Don't mess with her, dude."

"Uh, okay. Thanks man." Jake slams the door. Mick steps off the porch and walks down the sidewalk. *Down the street 2 blocks. Vegetarian. Well, that'll be okay for tonight. I hope they have beer. What a mess. Seriously... no more blind dates for me. Oh... there... those colorful banners. That must be the cafe.*

Realizmotron winds down.

Was that educational... or what? In exactly the same situation... humans can be counted on to respond totally differently. I'm sure you remember our earlier Realizmo scenario with the 4 young people and their completely different reactions as the sunbeam snake slithered across their path.

Let me just say... in the realm of being a human of Earth... relationship and communication... don't leave home without 'em.

Many humans grow up thinking success in their adult Life is all about money. Recognition. Accolades. More money. Perceived power. Stuff. Those misperceptions make for a brittle Life. There is so much more to human Life than money and stuff.

Developing caring, connected, loving relationships is a dimensionalizing realm of that *so much more*. "Love makes the world go 'round"... we've heard people say. That may even be a song. If it's not, it should be.

Mentioned several times thru-out your Orientation Moment... as you engage your Life while incarnate human... your psycho logicals will be busy sorting your experiences thru your own filters and attitudes. Creating beliefs. Thru these beliefs... like looking thru the window in your front door... you interpret everything you see, feel, and hear. The majority of the time... unless you are guided to "think for yourself"... your filters and attitudes will be those you inherited from others... your parents... friends... teachers... billboards... the internet.

The majority of humans find safety and justification in never questioning their own beliefs and attitudes. "Don't you dare challenge what I say!" To most it feels "safe" to completely believe "I am right!" This "I'm right!" stance... correct and all-knowing... never to be questioned... keeps humans frequently embroiled in dispute and argument. You'd think there was nothing better to do... think... feel.

Here's an insight into humanosity which will come as neither a shock nor a surprise... irrational belief structures are a driving force... a dividing force... in human nature.

Lousy impulse control... failure to resist temptation, urge, or fancy... has humans victimized by their own emotions... opinions... addictions. Messes get made. No one wants to clean them up. "*I* didn't make that mess!"

You will find... many humans go thru adult Life looking for their "father" to tell them what to do... and their "mother" to clean up after them. "Wait! What do you mean, *I'm* responsible? You think *I'm* going to clean this mess up?" Sometimes, this is physical mess. Many more times, it's emotional mess.

Many adult humans feel deeply threatened when their beliefs are questioned... religious... political... or otherwise. Clearly... this reaction reveals their personal insecurities. Their defensive tendencies. Rather than being able to have a conversation within differing opinions... often, there is a hot leap to anger and harsh words.

"Who are you to question *me*?!"

"That's stupid. You're wrong!"

"You're an idiot... sinner... hater... if you don't believe the same way I do!"

"Don't make me think about what I believe to be true!" (Unspoken fear: What if it turns out I'm wrong?) (What if there are additional aspects I should be considering?)

In short order... out comes the hostility and volatile artillery. The immediate go-to reaction for so many humans.

A truer statement would be... this is what is right *for me*. Cooler heads prevailing might say... "What I believe does not always have to be what's right for you."

But for many... it seems "you *have to* believe like me" is hard-wired. A reaction undoubtedly learned in their youngling years... as parents and other adult humans set the example... fixated on "I'm right! Don't question me!" "You better get with the program and say I'm right, too!" This is a throwback to the early stages of Instinct evolving into Intellect. The Instinct-Intellect self is wary of "others." Wary of others' thoughts and views. Wary of what's "different from me."

Unfortunately... many humans are intent upon passing their wary ways... their hatred and insecurities... along to future generations. "Remember, son... keep on hating the folks I've always hated."

Now I suggest you engage your Recall + Retain capacity as we reassess the power of potpourri on Planet Earth. There is a vast assortment of different. Different rocks and trees... fish and monkeys... cultures and contrivances. There are a gajillion different human beliefs and attitudes. Each human comes equipt with their own captivating set. Their own opinion kit. And intricately interwoven they are. As many different humans as there are... currently more than 7 billion and counting... there are that many different shades of belief and attitude. Quite an assortment. The nuances are profound. Sadly... so is the disdain and discord.

This contempt and strife shows up in every possible human realm... parents and their children (small, teen, and grown)... neighbors... coworkers... study groups... strangers. Where one or more humans are gathered... there resides likelihood for misunderstanding and conflict.

As we continue considering the realm of humans relating... I am reminded of another popular human phrase... "Would you rather be right, or would you rather be happy?" A person hanging on for dear Life to how "right" they are... often means their ears are shut and their brain is closed to what other people have to say. "I don't even want to hear it!" Rarely does this constricting, self-limiting, controlling stance lead to folks being happy.

It seems... many times, humans just want to make a fuss. And be right.

Do remember... you have a lot more available to experience as you are human than making a fuss. Or being right.

※ ※ ※

Emphasized thru-out your pre-incarnate Orientation... you've heard the human emotional nature is where the work lies. The truly dimensionalizing work of becoming a healthy, aware, resilient human.

This word, resilient… this way of being plays a significant role. Positive… beneficial… helpful… navigating your Life as a human of Earth. Your resilient emotional nature. The ability to change for the better. Not letting same ol' same ol'… "I've always done it this way"… calcified me… continue to rule the day. Moving beyond fossilized… out dated… snap judgment retorts. Just because hardened emotional arteries feel familiar doesn't mean they continue to serve you well.

Resilient denotes flexibility… robust… buoyant… strong… feisty, even. Recalibrating. Adjusting. Taking various internal and external factors into account. Not being only your previous rigid reactions. Fashioning your response. Choosing how you show up in your world.

Stretch. Breathe. Become.

This is the *real* "be all you can be."

As you are human, each body… physical, emotional, mental, spiritual… has its quirks… its own nuances and complexities. That truth is particularly profound in the human emotional nature. With that in mind… we will now focus on a few additional insights into human emotional Life. I believe you will find this useful.

The human Emotional Nature deserves special emphasis because:

1. It's murky in there. Shrouded with uncertainty... constrictions... harsh self-judgment. Self-neglect. Until the Light turns on... the human Emotional Nature is a dark, hurting place. Hidden in the dark are obstacle illusions... false beliefs... severe self-cruelty... for you to trip and fall over. Stumbling around, it is easy to get emotionally whacked and thrown off balance by your own fine self.
2. In potential, the human Emotional Body is the Clear, Light-Reflective Surface for the Light of the Soul. Attentive awareness is your ally as you begin to perceive and acquire this reality. Self-kindness is a wise compadre.
3. We are talking about humankind... The Pivotal 4th Kingdom. Pivotal within the well-being of the entire Planetary Life. The actual pivot resides within the human emotional nature. Humans are called upon to find their way to harmony and clear vision. Figuring out ways to express their differences constructively... moving beyond the snares of conflict and agitation. Finding their way back home.
4. There is much work to be done.

Shining light on this "work to be done"... let's expand on a few emotional survival procedures. Some of this you may have heard before. Adjust your Magic Decoder Ring. Engage your Recall + Retain Button. In the context of all you have experienced thru-out Orientation... you are going to find these highlights... these emoto insights... worth hearing again.

Here's a big one... as you are human, you, too, will find yourself riveted... engrossed within this paradoxical notion. Truthfully... it's a blight. Clogging the pipes of human perception. Humans believe, "I *am* my emotions." "I *am* my thoughts." "I am my beliefs... moods... attitudes... feelings." "I am my physical body... my looks... my fitness... my sense of style." As you are busy being human, you will grow up believing this about yourself. Eventually, as your awareness unfolds... you may grow beyond this flawed misperception. Or, it could be you'll ride it thru your entire incarnation.

Yes, you will have an emotional body. This does not mean you *are* your emotions. Yes... you will have a mental instrument... this does not mean you *are* your thoughts. *You* are not your physical body.

As Spirit living a human experience... you find yourself installed in an instrument... a vehicle thru which you engage your world. Similar to confusing the tea as its pot or the driver as their car. You are *not* your container. You are not your instrument. You have the ability to interact in your Life with thoughts and feelings. This does not mean *you* are those thoughts and feelings.

You are so much more.

That fascinating 3 body arrangement is yours to use. It does not use you.

As humans… walk… stumble… meander… race… thru Life… it seems many find comfort in not giving attention to their emotions. "What emotions? You mean *feelings*? Whoa… not me!" Too raw. Kinda scary. The Emotional Boogie Man ridin' the range.

For many, opening to emotion = feeling "out of control." Can't have that! Emotionally blind, humans plunge ahead… either steamrolling… or getting steamrolled. A steamroller is a slow-moving piece of heavy equipment used to flatten surfaces during road construction. "Flatten" being the operative word here. Many find heavy-handed tactics a convenient way to maneuver in their emotional Life. "Just flatten 'em. Run 'em right over!"

Yes, you're right… this approach does demonstrate a lack of finesse.

Here is a valuable tip: Resist focusing on how you've been wronged. Don't dwell.

Don't brood on imagined injustices. You will be tempted. Especially if you incarnate in "developed" countries… where, currently, some media outlets and TV stations manufacture a fraught environment as they preach grievance and division. "You've been wronged!" "They're out to get you!" "Be afraid. Be very afraid." Agitating. Incitement. Provocation. They brandish terrorizing false flags… preying on human fear. These folks make big money as they play on… play with… peoples' anxious insecurities.

Don't fall for it.

The angst of tormenting yourself over perceived slights and insults can seem so much "easier" than developing your own emotional nature and furthering your resilience. This self-invented angst is not the ally it pretends to be.

As you are being human… here is a question worth asking yourself: Why keep that painful turmoil… "I've been wronged!"… alive within you? Why keep scratching off those emotional scabs?

Taking up residence on Gripe Avenue is not where you want to live your inner Life. You'll end up with the worst sort of spiritual indigestion. All twisted and bitter. (Burp.) Why awfulize? Why focus on the worst?

Humans have a lot more going on for them than gripe and whine. Your ability to direct and finesse energies within your emotional self is much more available than you give yourself credit for.

Here is where developing your meditation practice serves you well. Meditating regularly helps you refine perspective. You won't immediately fall for every little conspiracy theory your thoughts and moods conjure up.

Another aspect to consider: Your human emotional component will experience "mixed feelings." You will find this to be true more than a few times. Being glad about something but feeling nervous at the same time. Being sad and yet relieved. Hating something, at the same time, acknowledging its benefit. A youngling going to Summer Camp for the first time... definitely excited... and trepidacious. Already missing Mom... yet, thrilled to be going out on their own.

On Planet Earth, mixed feelings will be ubiquitous... as in, found *everywhere*. Sadness as a loved one passes away... yet relieved they are no longer in pain. Huffing and puffing as you make yourself trudge up that hill every day... hating it. At the same time... "I gotta admit" the healthful physical benefit this arduous exercise brings. Life offering you a gift which you object to, yet still embrace.

Come here... come here. Get away... get away. Emotions. Mixed.

I see you nodding your heads. I am sure many of you are experiencing "mixed feelings" as you consider your upcoming entanglement with Life in human form. Even tho there is a surge of excitement... "Ohhh... I can hardly wait to see how this is all going to play out!" There is also realization… this upcoming endeavor is not always going to be a pretty picture. Or even that much fun.

When you've been out of incarnation for a while, it's easy to forget the emotional bumps and bruises. The struggle. The tussle. The suffering. Then… ta da!… you arrive at this moment on the brink of humanosity. The brink, indeed.

Time to "suit up." We're diving in again. Way in.

This next realization morsel is worth fully engaging your Recall + Retain Button. To note: Every other human will be having a Life experience different from yours. Even members of the same family have contrasting relationships with Life. Human beliefs… attitudes… opinions… who you perceive yourself to be… are all formulated by your experiences. And the way these Life experiences interact with the deep chemistry of your karmic fibres, awareness filters and rendezvous factors. Ever-influenced by your interpretation of these interactions. This individual stew with its various ingredients, herbs and spices, flavors what each person believes is "right."

There will be other people who believe… and expound… differently than you do. They are not "wrong." Just different. Different perceptions. Different Life-defining experiences. Different beliefs in how things should be. Different. Nothing to get in a huff about.

And yet, I do gotta say... getting in a huff does seem to come with the human territory. Huffiddy huff huff.

Upon observation... it's as if humans *want* to be upset and at odds with each other. Upset and at odds with their Life. This is identified as "unconscious" living. Oblivious, for sure. Is that really "easier?" Or is it just familiar?

Ever on the hunt... humans look for evidence. To prove... "My upset is valid!" "See *that*?! That proves it!" Convincing themselves... "My grievance... complaint... injustice... is the worst ever and requires immediate action! I have evidence! You better be convinced, too!"

Surveying matters currently playing out among Earth-tone humans... in the area of Earth known as the U.S. of A., it is curious to note... the generation of folks born after the end of "The 2nd Great War" came of age in a flurry of *Peace & Love*. Observing interesting choices made... they proceeded to age into the generation of "If you're not with us... you're against us."

"You don't idolize every word I say?!" "You dare scrutinize my actions and falsehoods!?" "Who cares if I repeatedly stiff my contractors?!" "You're not going to hold *me* accountable!"

As a group... this generation who started out wanting to save the planet... a startling number have aged into humans who, it seems, only want to save themselves. They set a self-absorbed, resource-consuming example which many thru-out the world are drawn to emulate. Their grasping, predatory stance cannot be sustained.

Their actions and agitating attitudes fall way short as a method to advance Planetary Well-Being.

At its core... this greedy arrogance fortifies the divide between humans. The many divides. Self-centered fixation keeps the rich rich and getting richer. As the poor are kept poor and getting poorer. This divide is fortified by self-serving complacency. The grasping human obsession with self-indulgence allows many to willfully turn a blind eye.

Entertainment. Comfort. Convenience. "Isn't this what Life is all about?"

To those accustomed to privilege, equality seems like oppression. "No! You will not disrupt my privilege just to make someone else's Life better!" "That's not right! I'm the victim here!"

A deeply entrenched sense of privilege creates its own toxic delusions. Humans have invented a term... "affluenza"... as a defense when the affluent do wrong. Insulated by their wealth and perceived specialness = their excuse to get away with harming others. To escape consequences. "Officer, I can't understand why what I did was wrong." "I'm too (rich) (well-connected) special to be held accountable... that's for the little people." At their behest… there's a special karmic picnic basket being readied just for them.

Let's look at another notable twist on "how things are." In our ongoing preparation itinerary for your upcoming Life… this has been mentioned previously. As you are actually being human… it won't take you long to catch on to this one. Many humans are highly reactive. They "take it personally." Whatever "it" might be. They are promptly offended by what other people say to them or about them. Defensive in a hot second. Like they stick their finger in an emotional electric socket. Folks get a big jolt. Immediately upset. Insulted. Busy interpreting another person's remarks or actions as a slight directed "against me!" Those hot buttons are *real* hot. Because, you know… "It's all about me!" "Are they insulting me?!"

Many times, the other person's intention is not to get someone riled up or offended. But, sure as shootin'… what is communicated gets received and reacted to with a pile of peeved. Their instant go-to reaction = "I'm so offended!" "Aggrieved!" Wronged. Frequently leaping to "You're going to pay for this!" Whoa… steady, big fella.

You will find there are some people who are ready to listen… clarify miscommunication… make amends.

Many humans plunge right into feeling hurt or attacked. In a heartbeat.

As you are entrenched in humanosity, do your best to remember... what someone says to you... or about you... reveals more about them than it does about you. The way other people express themselves or respond to what you say speaks of them... not you.

Choose to step away.

I know... I know. That approach... stepping away... not fighting back... is barely imaginable to some. Yet is there really any good reason to grab onto perceived hostility and activate it as your own? Is there any good reason to build on the irrational? (Uh... no.) Short-sighted comes to mind. "I only see what I want to see! And I'm right!" Blinded by the fight.

Enraged is an easy trap to leap into. "I'm going to explode!" (If I don't get my way!) Ok. Your choice.

I am not saying choosing not to engage... not to enrage... is an easy response. Not at first. For many humans, it's pretty tough. This takes serious, conscious choice. To even consider a less combustible approach. The tempest itself is so engaging. "I'm so mad!" So familiar. Engrossing. Then what? Mad, again. How's that feel? Where to from here?

Seriously... what is the value of raging? Combusting. Always ready to ignite and feel wronged. Vigilant in the search for who's "out to get me." Looking for who I'm supposed to hate.

Don't *ever* fall for… "It's your fault I'm so mad!" "You're *making* me… hit you… yell at you… belittle you!" No… you're not. The mad guy always wants to act like his/her raging is someone else's fault. "It's not my fault I'm so out of control!" Yes, it is.

When you are being human… as the perpetrator of this foolishness… it is *yours* to deal with. Stop acting like an idiot. Spraying your spew on loved ones and innocent bystanders alike. Nobody wants your steaming chunks of personal mismanagement. What are you afraid of? Anger… raging… is just fear's agitated cousin. Find yourself some anger management tools and resources. Use them. Take responsibility for your emotional outbursts. Stop blaming others.

If you are a victim of this false narrative… this blame game… do your best to understand you are *not* the reason for this toxic spew. In the heat of the moment… in the heat of another person's temper mental… it's easy to be swept right into believing it. Who knows… it may be safer, too… right then. But when the red hot moment has passed… do all you can to get yourself out of the situation or relationship. And, yes, I do realize that may be "easier said than done." So many complexities. Just do what you can to not swallow the falsehood… "*you* make me be this way." Not true.

Temper mental erases perspective… perception… and many other worthwhile considerations.

Steaming in your "I'm so mad" fogs your lens. Distorts your view of your world. And who you are in this moment. You're not seeing clearly.

Could there be other emotional options to explore? There could be.

There are.

You... *choosing* within yourself... who you are going to be... *how* you are going to be. That's a possibility. An option. Let's face it... the storm... the temper mental tempest... does not always have to win.

Game on.

You *are* emotionally capable to adjust your irritability. To repurpose the energies acting out in your rage tornado. Let your personal energies be something else in you. Allow them (you) to show up differently. You don't always have to be duped by your own bad behavior. Carrying on in the crash and bash of your emotional tsunami is not a requirement of your being human agreement.

Draw a deep, centering breath. Draw a few more.

Give yourself a break.

Decide to grab the reins of your untethered emotional stallion.

As you decide to make different inner choices... the dark storm clouds begin to part. The dawn emerges. Opening to other possible ways to respond sets the stage for these other possibilities to be… possible.

Other possibilities, you say? Well, yes, in fact there are. Many.

There is always *not* enraging. Cut that immediate, knee jerk reaction off at the pass. Just shut it. Ok… that's different. Worthy of consideration.

Draw another deep, centering breath. And another. Let's explore other likelihoods for your success. Here's one viable option… choose to develop and exercise your more Life-affirming emotional muscles. Perhaps begin by noticing things in your Life you are grateful for. A rewarding practice. Take yourself in that direction.

There's always this current popular phrase which does a good job summing up aspects of this human dynamic: "What you think of me is none of my business." *Touchè*.

Whatever you may say or do… other humans will react the way they react. They just will. Don't grab onto another person's snit as your own. Don't stab yourself with it. In any exchange… there is your part… and there is their part. You expressing your beliefs and opinions… that's "your part." What comes out of someone else's mouth… the way they express… how they react to what you say… that's "their part."

Humans are way too inclined to get their panties in a twist. Being all offended… hot and bothered… by someone else's reactions or behavior. Hypervigilant to feeling messed with. Hypervigilant to being "right."

When you are human… being perpetually miffed… revved-up and irritated… is not good for your well-being. Hard on your joints. Grinds your teeth. Disrupts digestion. Fritzes your wiring.

Choose your battles.

Oh, while we're rambling around in emoto world… here's another point worth noting: Do not fool yourself thinking you can "fix" or "change" *anybody*. That's called "meddling." Many people get way too consumed… with their nose all up in another person's business. Of course, you feel you are "right" as you offer your suggestions. Your "constructive criticism." You *know* their Life would be better off if they just did what *you* think they should do.

Don't be The Disapprover. It's not as much fun… as "right"… as you might think.

Really… back away. Let the people in your Life experience their Life as they want to… warts and all. Just as you surely want other people to let you live your Life as you see fit… warts and all.

All that criticism and reproach. Disapproval. It is the easiest thing to criticize. To point out every wrong thing. "I completely disapprove." "This is *wrong*." And this. And this.

"Constructive" or otherwise… criticism makes the critic feel "right." Spot-on. Justified. All kinda uppity. Perhaps to the other person… all kinda not so "constructive." All kinda fault-finding. Why be any degree of understanding… helpful or beneficial… when it's so much easier to criticize?

As humans go about participating in this particular realm of the Game of Life… there seems to be a short supply of "Let It Be."

One true sign of an evolving emotional nature is being genuinely happy when something good happens to someone else. "I'm so happy this good thing happened for you!" Many people take another person's good as an assault to their own identity and well-being. "That should be mine!" "How come all the good things happen to her?" "I'm the one who deserves that!" "Why don't I get any of the good stuff?"

Well… you're living *your* Life. They're living theirs.

Being envious of another person's good does not bring good to you. It only makes you feel unhappy… grumpy… bummed out… about your own Life. When you first start practicing being happy for another person's good… it might feel kind of "clunky." Unnatural. Like any other muscle… it takes time. Exercise. It's well worth the effort. In ways you are not even able to imagine.

Spare yourself unnecessary emotional wear and tear. Be happy for another person's good. Riding your merry-go-round of Life will be so much merrier.

There's another item I want to reiterate as our Orientation draws to a close: "Is-ness." Simply what *is*. The human psyche... that ultra-wise, kinda sassy, clearly deranged thinkery/emoto combo... strives to justify and explain. Comes up with ways to "figure things out." By creating story. Many times, the human story around "what is" rocks with reactive elements... making events "good"... "I am so lucky!" Or "bad"... "This is horrible. Why is this happening to me?"

There is "what *is*"... and there's all the stuff folks instantaneously make up about "what is." As you are a growing, evolving human... it won't even occur to you to simply reside within "what is." You will automatically make stuff up. You will come up with commentary and configuration... to supplement... judge... augment... any situation or occurrence. Humans usually gyrate somewhere on the spectrum between "This is really great!" and "This totally sucks."

Most people harbor an attachment to sculpt any situation into... "how this should be"... "what I want to have happen." Quick to tag what *is* happening as "this isn't what I want." "This isn't *it*!"

Here's an item that will not naturally occur to your

human self... there is no need to accessorize the moment.

At some point, you will wake up to the reality... I can simply be good with what *is*. I don't need to be running off making "what is" glorious or poopy. I have options. Settle into the moment. Observe. Stretch. Embrace. Be satisfied.

This ability to be in the is-ness brings you gifts of peace and balance. Harmony, even.

The moment... unadorned by judgment, fluff or panic... may show itself to be more of a revelation than you could have anticipated.

In a situation or relationship, it may seem an odd notion to simply observe what *is* going on. This is superb exercise. *Is what is.* Brings you into this current moment. To see things as they *are*. With practice... the world you live in will look and feel like a place transformed.

Here's another point I am inspired to add... Life is not a race. And it is certainly not a competition.

Competition... rivalry = just another human construct. Unless you are The Winner... whatever that means... competition mostly makes folks feel bad. "Not good enough." Less than "#1." At odds... in their own Life.

In human Life the only real competition is with yourself.

Strive to be your best incarnant self. Make the most of the time you have. This prime opportunity to excel at *your* version of The Game of Life.

You be *you*. Rock on.

Remember... The *Path* Is The Goal. There is no "there." No destination. No trophy at the finish line. No finish line. Who cares who "the winner" is? That's all made up stuff. More of those dustbin details.

You will be walking *your* Path. How well you do you is what counts. How awake and aware you become in your human time allotted. How kind and contributing you are with the other lives you touch.

Show up. Be kind. Contribute.

Well, my fine compadres... as the charming Beatles' song goes... "Now it's time to say good night." Your Orientation Moment here at The Interpretorium is complete. It has truly been a pleasure being your Tour Guide. I know you will have one rock 'em, sock 'em human incarnation on Planet Earth! Go get 'em, Sparky!

Please do connect with me when you return here to pure cognizance. I'd love to hear how it all goes.

Remember... living a human Life without developing your awareness is like shooting blanks.

Again, let me say...

   Your mission... should you choose to accept it:
   Wake up as soon as possible while in human form.

Cheers.

CHAPTER FOUR

" <u>13</u> "
Dare To Take The Step

*"Or... attitude being everything...
you could say, here's where the fun begins."*

Earlier in *Holy Wow!*, I mentioned… The Nature of The Soul training and my time at Nyingma truly set my feet upon my Path in this incarnation. Both of these Life-transforming opportunities presented themselves to me in my early 20s. They are delectably intertwined. I brought myself to Nyingma due to the suggestion and kind generosity of Lucille Cedercrans, the woman who created The Nature of The Soul material.

I see this now… The Nature of The Soul planted many seeds of awareness possibility. Nyingma provided the garden... the nourishing ground... for those seeds to take root. Experiences as I lived at Nyingma... presented whisps of past Life recall... enriching and fertilizing my growing realizations.

I am beyond blessed. Grateful to have received such insights, knowledge, and experiences at such a young age. I savor that time. Those moments and interactions... their gifts of insight and realization... are vibrant silken cords woven deeply thru-out the tapestry of my Life.

The Nyingma tradition is the oldest of the four major schools of Tibetan Buddhism. Amazingly... the Tibetan alphabet and written grammar were created specifically to translate Buddhist scriptures from the Sanskrit. Talk about inspired motivation! The written Tibetan language came into being for the purpose of translating what was then a new way of being. A new way of seeing our world. That's admirable. Inspired. Pretty cool.

In Tibetan sacred art called *thangkas* (TAWN kuhs)... you will frequently see a two-headed bird... representing the translator. Warm acknowledgment is given to those who provided this gift of the Dharma to the Tibetan people. Translating... like a singing bird... from Sanskrit to the language of the Tibetans.

Based on those first translations, Nyingma was established in the 8th century CE.

As part of my right livelihood during the months I lived at Nyingma... I worked at Dharma Publishing.

Keenly aware of Tibet's irreparable losses... Dharma Publishing sustains the precious spiritual heritage from the Land of Snows. Their work preserves Tibetan art and texts... distributing texts to Tibetan monks and scholars... publishing Tibetan Buddhist books in Western languages. They communicate the meaning and value of The Dharma. In this case, The Dharma refers to the truth Buddha revealed and his teachings... the Middle Way... the 4 Noble Truths... the Eightfold Path... among many others.

Under the guidance of Tarthang Tulku Rinpoche... Dharma Publishing preserves and distributes these ancient Tibetan texts. Holding this vision... a day will come when this precious enlightened knowledge will once again be fully applied for the benefit of all Humankind.

My transportation from Nyingma to Dharma Publishing... zipping along on the back of a motorcycle. Driven by another young woman thru the streets of Berkeley to Oakland, where the publishing house was located. Come rain or come shine... whizzing along. Makes me smile... remembering.

A treasure I've kept with me from my time at Nyingma is actually a paper advert for a book they published at that time, *The Natural Freedom of Mind*... based on the works of Long Chen Pa... a major teacher of the Nyingma tradition since the 1300s. My treasure reads:

> "Since everything is but an apparition
> perfect in being what it is,
> having nothing to do with good or bad
> acceptance or rejection,
> one may well burst out in laughter."

Indeed, one may well.

Which makes me think of a greeting card by the gifted artist, Mary Englebreit. This card was my go-to stationary thru the '80s. A lively court jester dances on the front of the card with the words:

"Life's Too Mysterious... Don't Take It Serious."

I'll say.

Both of these "friendly reminders"... "One may well burst out in laughter" and "Don't take it serious"... are deeply woven into my Life tapestry. As I mentioned... I inherited a pretty easy-going nature from my Dad. These 2 "suggestions" remind me to, indeed, go easy.

While we are talking about treasures... I'm going to share with you my favorite Buddha story. Beginning with a little backstory.

As Buddha sat under the Bodhi tree... he was not looking to ponder the great secrets of the universe with his intellect. As Buddha reached toward enlightenment... it was not his mind that expanded and became clear. It was his heart.

His Being.

Enlightenment and true transformation occur... as our *emotional* nature is balanced, explored, and called to its highest. Boogie Man be gone!

Relax the frightened vigilance of your emotions. Disengage from fear. Release yourself from fear of reprimand. The fear of being punished or penalized. The fear of being seen as "doing it wrong."

What if you're actually doing it right?

Drop your conflict... which no longer serves you. The fabrication of self-incited drama evaporates. Realization of the spacious grace of The Love That Heals grants limitless understanding. Peace.

Generosity of Spirit prevails.

Thanks, Goodness... for that.

And now... my favorite Buddha story:

> Having attained enlightenment,
> Buddha radiated an ineffable glow.
> Three holy men came along the path.
> Astounded by the brilliance of his luminous stature,

> one of them asked, "Are you a god?"
> Buddha replied, "No."
> Another asked, "Are you a saint?"
> "No."
> "What *are* you then?"
> "I am awake."

Thus he attained the title *Buddha*... "The Awakened One."

These 3 holy men were part of the group of ascetics Buddha lived with for the 6 years before his awakening. Together, they practiced the rigors of self-denial... strict austerities and self-mortification... which supposedly would lead to Nirvana. After living these years of sincere, intense spiritual practice... it became clear... this was not the way to find answers to deep seeking and questioning.

Naturally, Buddha has an "origin story" just like the story of Jesus in his manger with the brilliant guiding star and the 3 wise men. There are many fascinating omens and portent to Buddha's story... including his mother's dream and a white bull elephant.

A very brief overview of his early Life... Siddhartha Gautama, the man who became Buddha, was the only son of a king. Growing up, his father made sure he lived an insulated Life... surrounded by luxury... free from difficulty and conflict. With no awareness of the suffering of others. His father kept him sheltered… wanting him to grow up to be King and a leader of men.

Yet, Siddhartha felt drawn to learn more about the struggles of Life outside his compound walls. He snuck out. His awareness… his Life… was transformed by the hardships, sickness and death he saw.

Later, as he engaged in those austere practices… Siddhartha came to the realization… there must be a middle way between the extremes of a Life of luxury and the extremes of a Life of austerity.

Watching the playing of a lute… a guitar-like instrument… Buddha realized… if the strings of the lute are wound too tight... music cannot be played... the instrument can even become damaged by the stress. If the strings are too slack… music cannot be played... the loose strings do not carry the lyrical notes. Thus, Buddha encouraged seeking the Middle Way as we live our lives. Straining too hard may damage your instrument. Being too lax does not bring you the sweet music of Life you are looking for.

In the Middle Way, we each find balance and harmony.

Buddha did become a leader of men… and women… just not in the way his father had anticipated.

The purpose of Lord Buddha's teachings? To tame the wild stallion of the mind. You know that stallion. Rapidly rushing mind… racing all over the place. Here. There. Everywhere. Overthink run amok. Wild with stinkin' thinkin'.

Buddha wisely declared… "Your worst enemy cannot harm you as much as your own unguarded thoughts."

The illumined state of Nirvana… being free from afflictions which arise from wrong thought. From wrong perception.

Following his enlightenment… Buddha spent 7 weeks in retreat and meditation. How would he share the insights and realizations that had come to him? Both the miraculous and the ordinary. He was not sure.

As per my "favorite Buddha story"… in time, he reconnected with the group of ascetics he once struggled with… in their rigid, rigorous quest to attain enlightenment. Knowing they were still steeped in the meaningless rigors of their extreme asceticism… he invited these monks to become his first students.

In the realm of "first things first"… Buddha's earliest teachings were about the cessation of suffering. In sharing his Four Noble Truths… Buddha taught that suffering could become extinct.

The Four Noble Truths:

> There is suffering.
> Suffering arises from grasping…

attachment to desires and wrong perceptions.
There is a way out of suffering...

suffering ceases as attachment to desire ceases.
There is freedom from suffering.

"Freedom from suffering" leads us to The Eight-Fold Path... the practice of Right Action... Right Mindfulness... Right Livelihood... plus others. Emphasis on "practice." The way to freedom does not lie in scholarly study and intellectualizing. The way to freedom is found thru meditation. Mindfulness. Practice. Thru *living* these teachings.

Buddha's teachings are not about suffering. Buddha's teachings are about releasing your self from suffering. This is the ultimate freedom while you are incarnate in human form.

And his teachings are about exuberance! The truth that this freedom is available... accessible... to all. WooHoo!

Do you know why Buddha would not make a good vacuum cleaner salesman? Too many attachments.

What did Buddha say to the hot dog vendor? "Make me one with everything."

It is said... "Strive to be a Buddha, not a Buddhist!"

I was raised in the Christian tradition... Baptist and Methodist. On Glenoaks Boulevard in Burbank, California... the Baptist Church and the Methodist Church were one block from each other. When I was a young child...

my parents and I attended the Baptist Church... which was my father's childhood persuasion.

Some sort of "scandal" happened involving the minister at the Baptist Church... which offended my mother. So, from the time I was 11... we attended the Methodist Church... the religion my mother had grown up in. I like the Christian tradition. But sometimes, people who strongly identify as Christian seem to love God... but not their fellow humans. Judgement abounds... provoking an "us or them" mentality. Which benefits neither "us" nor "them."

I have noticed many times... in more than one religious persuasion... ministers and leaders in the church fan the flames of that "us or them" dynamic. Preaching this contingency or that group are "against us." Like cooking up all the folderol around whether someone says "Happy Holidays" or "Merry Christmas." Really? Here we have warm, good wishes being offered... why get fussed and snappish about vocabulary? Why busily conjure variations on feeling belittled or disrespected? Building and fostering a culture of grievance. Conjuring supposed slights. Looking for injury. "We have to unite against those who are against us. We must fight!" This dynamic of contempt for others... of advancing antagonism... seems perceived by some as a successful way for ministers to herd their flock.

Why busily concoct your own ripple in The Force?

Let us each... and together... find ways to increase who's "us." Let's grow the "us" club. As we consciously choose to decrease who we perceive as "them." Ultimately, this is a karmic agreement. "I will be one who fosters unity and our common well-being." Rather than blindly continuing age-old patterns which fester disagreement and discord. We can make this the choice. We *can* be better.

The Dalai Lama says, "All religions have the potential to create better human beings... but no one religion can claim supremacy over the other."

You may recall, in Volume II, I mentioned the pleasure of seeing Senator Cory Booker speak in Washington, DC in early 2016. (This was before either Senator Booker or his friend and moderator, Secretary of Housing and Urban Development Julian Castro, became 2020 Democratic Presidential candidates.) One reason I was interested in seeing Senator Booker... was a post of his I read... and saved... from Facebook. Cory Booker wrote:

> "Before you speak to me about your religion,
> first show it to me in how you treat other people;
> before you tell me how much you love your God,
> show me in how much you love all His children.

"Before you preach to me of your passion for your faith,
teach me about it thru your compassion
for your neighbors.
In the end, I'm not as interested in
what you have to tell or sell
as in how you choose to live and give."

The clear insight of these words speaks to me.

I definitely resonate with the Christ energy. I have had my own personal interactions with Jesus. A memory prominent in my mind as I write this... ushered into a room in the medical clinic where I would learn of my breast cancer diagnosis, I sat on the exam table, waiting for the doctor to come in. All of a sudden... to my surprise... Jesus was standing right in front of me. Three of his angel friends stood off to my right. These were not fancy angels with big, shining wings. They were dressed simply... as was Jesus. They just stood with me as I sat on the exam table... waiting. I was deeply touched. Awash in a centering, peace-filled energy. Which, of course, in that moment, I much appreciated. I did, however, get the sense... the news the doctor was bringing would not be "benign."

Even in my youth... it seemed to me the various religions of the world were not that different. Of course... appearances and rituals differ. But each religion speaks of Love.

Compassion. Kindness. Good works. They are each mythologies. Explaining traditions. Bringing their constituents a sense of hope, belonging, and community. Including, hopefully, a soul-enriching perception of the world around them.

In groups and retreats as I speak of religions and Spirit... I frequently use the metaphor of wells and the water which fills them. People can get pretty wrapped up in how that well is supposed to look and where it should be located.

"Your well had better be under a tall oak tree and be made of rounded river rock and stand 4 feet tall... or it's not a real well!"

"Your well has to look like my well... made of wood... 2 feet tall, with palm trees all around."

And yet... the true significance is not the well... but the water. The Spirit inside. All of the wells are as they are. Located where they are to make the water available to drink. What the well looks like does not make its water any more or less watery.

I was coming from my Christian background as I first encountered meditation and The Nature of The Soul. In the early '70s, after teaching my initial round of The Nature of The Soul... I went on my first road trip to Oregon. At that time... the author of this Life-transforming material, Lucille Cedercrans, was living in a suburb of Portland. I reached out to her and we became friends.

During one of our far-ranging conversations, she told me it was clear to her that The Nature of The Soul... which she had written 20 years earlier, in the mid-50s... was a blend of Christian and Hindu philosophies. In the mid-60s... she began her study of Buddhism. As we talked... Lucille told me she wished she had realized more about Buddhism when she was writing The Nature of The Soul. She would have woven more heart-centered, compassionate self-awareness into The Nature of The Soul material.

By the time Lucille and I were having these conversations... she had already studied with Tarthang Tulku and other Buddhist scholars. Lucille was the first woman from the West recognized as an incarnate lama... a *tulku*... in her own right. As I mentioned at the beginning of this chapter... it was Lucille's guidance and generosity that took me to Nyingma. She encouraged me to go there and kindly made available her suite of rooms in the compound for me to live in.

I arrived at Nyingma in my early 20s. Here began my study and admiration of Buddhism. I was not renouncing my Christian roots. It did not occur to me there could be even a smidge of conflict. As far as I can tell... Buddha and Jesus... each 6th Kingdom Avatars... get along just fine. They're friends. Right compatible, even. It would not occur to them to be in conflict about the different religions which have grown up around their teachings. Their Presence.

As I said... it didn't occur to me, either.

During my time at Nyingma and thru-out my adult Life... I would recall Lucille telling me, as I mentioned... how, at the time she originally transcribed her teaching materials... she wished her instrument had been more attuned to the Buddhist understanding of the workings of heart and mind. Her sharing that with me, guided me to be more open to those Life perspectives as they came my way. As they unfolded before me.

A fascinating tenant of Buddhism... there is no focus on worshipping a particular individual or deity. In Buddhist focus and development... awareness dawns on our human capability to move ourselves beyond... our anxiety and insecurity... our blame and overthink. How we can make choices and take steps to move beyond our suffering. Taming the wild stallion.

Buddhism guides us to learn about ourselves. Remembering who we are. Living Life with greater mindfulness. With more insightful awareness and compassion. With greater joy.

Ever since living at Nyingma... I have felt what I can best describe as a buoyant resonance with the Dalai Lama. Many years ago, I came across a card with a lovely black and white photo of the Dalai Lama on the front. Inside, the card says, "My religion is kindness." Reading that, I thought, "Mine, too."

Pictures of the Dalai Lama are all around my home... here and there... large and small. Friendly reminders. For me... just seeing his face = Ahhhh. Thanks for being here on Planet Earth. We are lucky to be here, aren't we? Such a good thing.

In 1995... my son, Isaiah, traveled to Dharamsala, India, with a group from his high school. Dharamsala is the residence of the Dalai Lama along with thousands of Tibetans and the Tibetan Government in exile. Isaiah and his fellow students came to help build a school. They were also there for the celebration of the Dalai Lama's 60th birthday.

Isaiah gifted me with the white silk scarf... the *khata*... the Dalai Lama had placed around his neck in a traditional Tibetan ceremonial gesture of acknowledgment. I was completely delighted to receive it. As Isaiah bowed his head before me, gently placing that snowy white scarf around my neck... I cried. I figured, "This is the closest I am going to get to the Dalai Lama in this Life." Totally fine by me.

I always knew I would help my parents "in some way" as they aged. This was the closest my "previews of coming attractions" ever got as I would think about that particular aspect of my Life. Then events transpired. As it became clear my mother was in mental decline... my father had his first stroke. Here it is... our call to action. Scott and I began our preparations to move from our home in Portland, Oregon, into my childhood bedroom in Southern California to care for my parents. The previous "in some way" had arrived.

I was fine with this development of moving to help my folks. But, I gotta tell ya... this was 26 years after my first fateful road trip to Oregon and the unfolding of my Life there... I was not thrilled with the idea of living in SoCal again. I was grumbling to myself about this one day when a voice in my head said... "I'm *sure* something good will come of this!"

I had heard this very distinctive voice a few times before. She is always right. I say "she" because the tone of the voice... high-pitched and lilting... sounds like Glinda, The Good Witch of the North, from *The Wizard of Oz*. She chimes in, all optimistic... with her emphasis on *sure*. "I'm *sure* something good will come of this!"

And again... she was right. In the 10 years Scott and I lived in Southern California, many wonderful things happened for us. Including... A#1 for me... I got to study with the Dalai Lama 3 times. Me and about 1,000 other people. On 3 different occasions, at the Pasadena Civic Auditorium. Altho I do feel a connexion with Tibetan Buddhism... I am not a Tibetan Buddhist in this Life. I deeply admire and resonate with the teachings. But, sitting in that auditorium... I was there for the Dalai Lama.

I was there to breathe the same air.

Just to be in the same space and time with him. Just to release into his vibration. It was sublime. I was sublimed.

The 2nd time I was there... I sat in row 'I'... 9 rows back from the stage... directly in front of the Dalai Lama. Beauteous. Grace. Holy Moley. I soaked it up.

Recognized as an embodiment of the Bodhisattva of Compassion... the Dalai Lama refers to himself as "a simple monk." Tibetan Buddhists refer to him as *Kundun*... "Presence."

The Dalai Lama frequently states his Life is guided by 3 major commitments:

1. The promotion of basic human values or secular ethics in the interest of human happiness
2. The fostering of inter-religious harmony
3. The preservation of Tibet's Buddhist culture... a culture of peace and non-violence.

He has said...

"Be kind whenever possible. It is always possible."

"Happiness is not something ready-made.
It comes from your own actions."

"This is my simple religion.
There is no need for temples;

no need for complicated philosophy.
Our own brain, our own heart is our temple;
the philosophy is kindness."

Here, to me, is the essence of the Buddhist perspective. This is The Bodhisattva Vow... from Shantideva, a revered 8th-century Indian Buddhist monk:

For as long as space endures,
and for as long as living beings remain
until then may I, too, abide
to dispel the misery of the world.

Some people may read those words and go, "Huh?" Others read that vow and feel an ocean of calm wash thru them.

At the beginning of 2017... our longtime friend, Joy, gifted me a copy of *The Book of Joy*... published by Avery-Penguin-Random House. This is a gently amazing book. In it, author Douglas Abrams recounts conversations on joy between His Holiness the 14th Dalai Lama and Archbishop Desmond Tutu. As you can imagine... these are wondrous and worthwhile conversations.

Each of these men grew up in challenge, difficulty, and struggle. Each has come to his deep understanding of joy thru harsh experience. Each of these remarkable men found joy thru his own choices... his own training... his own decisions. Joy and understanding were not just handed to either of them. Each developed his ability to choose joy and happiness in the context of a Life of rigor and difficulty.

Born in July, 1935... the Dalai Lama was recognized at age 2... as *tulku*... the reincarnation of the 13th Dalai Lama. His enthronement ceremony as the Dalai Lama was in February, 1940. At age 4. In 1950, as the nascent People's Republic of China invaded Tibet... he was installed as the spiritual leader of the Tibetan people. He was 15.

China had its sights set on Tibet. Despite many centuries of autonomous history... Mao Tse Tung's government insisted Tibet was not its own country. Mao considered Tibet a province of China. (Truth be told: China wanted the land... specifically to weaponize the strategic heights of the Himalayas.)

In 1959, the conflict and brutality dramatically escalated. With many Tibetans fearing for his Life... the young Dalai Lama, disguised as a soldier, fled Tibet. After a long and arduous trek over the 19,000 foot peaks and snow-covered mountain passes of Tibet... enduring snowstorms and sandstorms... he and his retinue escaped into exile in India.

Desmond Tutu was the first black Archbishop of Cape Town. He was born in 1931. Archbishop Tutu is an international social rights activist and the Anglican Archbishop Emeritus of Southern Africa. He grew up... a person of color... during the very difficult... searing... time of apartheid.

As an adult, he was a prominent leader in the struggle for justice and racial reconciliation in South Africa. Archbishop Tutu is deeply admired by many. From the intense cauldron of apartheid conflict... he pioneered a new way for countries to move forward after having experienced great civil conflict and unjust oppression. He is the founding chair of The Elders... a group of world leaders working together to promote peace and human rights.

Archbishop Tutu and the Dalai Lama consider each other "my mischievous spiritual brother."

Douglas Abrams, founder and president of Idea Architects, has worked with Desmond Tutu as his cowriter and editor for more than a decade. Mr. Abrams writes the narration of *The Book of Joy*... recounting the Dalai Lama's and the Archbishop's teachings on joy... along with their interactions and conversations.

A prominent element in *The Book of Joy* is the latest science on joy. Mr. Abrams notes, "With new discoveries in brain science and experimental psychology, there are now many profound insights into human flourishing."

Humans *flourishing*. As it should be.

Douglas Abrams also writes, "We were in search of true joy that was not dependent on the vicissitudes of circumstance. In this book, I have tried to share with you their intimate conversations, which were filled with seemingly endless laughter and punctuated by many poignant moments of recalling love and loss. Their joy is clearly not easy or superficial but one burnished by the fire of adversity, oppression, and struggle. They shared their hard-won wisdom of how to live with joy in the face of Life's inevitable sorrows."

Here, I will weave together for you some of their insightful comments from *The Book of Joy*.

Joy is our essential nature... something everyone can realize. Our innate desire for happiness is an attempt to rediscover our original state of mind. Our original state of being. Buddhists believe joy is our natural state. And, the ability to experience joy can be cultivated as a skill. Exploring joy is exploring what makes human experience satisfying.

In exercising our joy muscles... Archbishop Tutu says, "Perhaps we are just more alive. Yet as we discover more joy... we can face suffering in a way that ennobles rather than embitters. We have hardship without becoming hard. We have heartbreak without being broken."

The Dalai Lama points out... "Too much self-centered thinking is the source of suffering. A compassionate concern for others' well-being is the source of happiness. All dharma teachings agree on one point... lessening one's self-absorption."

Lessening one's self-absorption. "What about me?" "What about mine?" So much of human suffering occurs within our own head and heart. So much depends on where we put our attention. Am I fixated on my own suffering? Or am I compassionate... empathetic... to the suffering of others? (How can I help?)

Do we focus on our perceived separation? Or do we recognize our indivisible connexion?

How we choose to act each day is what matters.

Our suffering is so often self-inflicted. The Dalai Lama calls avoiding suffering and discovering happiness the very "purpose of Life." He goes on to say... "The ultimate source of happiness is within us. Not money, not power, not status. Some of my friends are billionaires, but they are very unhappy people. Power and money fail to bring inner peace. Outward attainment will not bring real inner joyfulness. We must look inside."

The 2 men talked about the continuing difficulties in Tibet and the sadness the Dalai Lama felt about what was happening to his cherished homeland. They also spoke of the challenges of perpetuating the Tibetan Buddhist way of Life... which is in great peril.

Earlier in this chapter, I quoted The Bodhisattva Vow... the words of the ancient Indian teacher, Shantideva. Regarding the Dalai Lama's ongoing exile and his concerns for his people... Archbishop Tutu asked him, "Why are you not morose?" In response... the Dalai Lama shared a practice he uses from Shantideva:

> "If something can be done about the situation,
>   what need is there for dejection?
> And if nothing can be done about it,
>   what use is there for being dejected?"

The Dalai Lama went on to paraphrase... "When you experience some tragic situation, think about it. If there's no way to overcome the tragedy, then there is no use worrying too much."

The Archbishop laughed. This almost seemed too incredible. Someone could stop worrying just because it was pointless to worry? He responded... "I think people know this with their head. You know that it doesn't help worrying. But they still worry." Archbishop Tutu went on to say... "The thing is, don't feel guilty. We have no control over our feelings. Emotions are spontaneous things that arise."

As I was reading *The Book of Joy*, I noticed... and Douglas Abrams also commented... "This was a point that the Archbishop and the Dalai Lama would disagree on during the week: How much control do we have over our emotions? The Archbishop would say we have very little. The Dalai Lama would say we have more than we think."

My inquiry would be... how well do most humans know themselves emotionally? Emotional self-understanding makes a tremendous difference in how we feel inside. And, especially, in how we are able to interact with our world and the people in it.

Buddhists practice focused inquiry... into how we humans operate. How we are able to direct our thoughts. And lift our hearts. The fruits of that inquiry = what we learn about ourselves and how we function. This practice definitely sheds light on the spectrum between... "we know very little"... and "we have more influence over our emotions than we may think."

Yes... here we see another *spectrum* in human reality. One pole... "we cannot direct our emotions." The opposite pole... "sure we can." And everything transpiring in between. Oh, *that* spectrum. You see it unfolding from... emotions as Boogie Man. Then, drawing a deep breath. Taking a moment to look within. Personal inquiry. Awareness of one's self. Clarity revealed. Choices made. Response-ability. To... Life is good.

It was actually noticing this spectrum... these emotional insight "poles"... that led me to include reference to *The Book of Joy* here in *Holy Wow!*

I observed… the Archbishop seemed to say, time and again… being aware of and directing our emotional energy is really more than can be expected of a human being. This belief is the result of the Christian tradition not training its flock in competent emotional ways and means. Not highlighting the tools of healthy personal inquiry and well-being. This I say without judgment… simply observation.

All the while the Dalai Lama is saying… of course we can be more aware. We should be more aware. We *must* be more aware.

This is the path of a practicing Buddhist:

Become aware of the emotional effect you are having inside yourself. The inner emotional environment you create and live within.

Be aware of the effect you are having on those around you. The outer emotional environment you create and thru which you touch your world.

Teach yourself to be more inclined to figure it all out in a mindful, harmonious way.

Proceed accordingly.

Meditating… looking within… developing healthy self-awareness… is not the "navel gazing" it has blithely been labeled by those who have no idea what they're talking about. Those who have no experience in this practice... no inkling of understanding. Blathering in the weakness of ridicule... they belittle what they do not know. Their flippant comments reveal only their own ignorance.

A person makes the time to "inquire within"... looking into their own ways of being... in the interest of becoming healthier... more authentic and well-balanced. Choosing to cultivate interaction with the world... and the people in it... in a more capable, congenial way. Developing a personal awareness which adds to the well-being of people and situations. Rather than childishly and churlishly stirring up difficulty and discord.

Reading *The Book of Joy*... I appreciated Douglas Abrams' recounting 2 different psychological studies and what they concluded. The first was a 1978 landmark study which found... long-term... lottery winners were not that much happier than people who had been paralyzed in an accident.

Say what!?!

From this study and subsequent work on cultivating happiness... the understanding has developed... people have a "set point" which determines their happiness over the course of their Life. An event or development occurs that "makes us happy"... and we're "happy." Once we get used to this new "happy"... we return to our general state of happiness. Our "set point." In many cases, a person's "set point" might be kind of glum. Not all that exuberant.

(Rereading that statement about "our general state of happiness"… the thought occurs… could exercising gratitude have anything to do with this? Hmmmm…)

Mr. Abrams also shared the work of psychologist Sonja Lyubomirsky, whose studies suggest… only about 50 percent of our happiness is determined by factors like our genes or temperament… our "set point." The other half of our happiness is determined by a combination of… our circumstances… in which we may have limited control… and our attitudes and actions… over which we should be able to have more control.

According to Lyubomirsky's work… there are 3 factors which seem to have the greatest influence on increasing our happiness:

1. Our ability to re-frame our situation more positively
2. Our ability to express gratitude
3. Our choice to be kind and generous.

What do you know?! These are exactly the attitudes and actions the Dalai Lama and Archbishop Tutu mentioned as central pillars of joy. Check. Check. And check.

There is much awareness and insight to be found in *The Book of Joy*. Definitely a worthwhile read. Especially as we endeavor to become more aware and skilled in creating a Life that hums. A Life that contributes. A Life that lifts well-being. Both our own and others'.

This brings me to share with you something I noticed a good while back. We all are here to learn our lessons and basically "lighten up." We're here to remember. We're here to be happy. When you encounter a person who professes to be a Spiritual Teacher... and they look all grim and serious... the question arises... is this person truly enlightened? Have they, indeed, "(en)lightened up?" Could they truly have something worthwhile to teach you? Or are they all puffed up and serious with their own self-importance? Does this teacher want you to know how tough and stern the spiritual journey is? In their presence, do you feel judged and not worthy... not holy enough? (Spoiler alert... Where's their joy?)

✥ ✥ ✥

I'm going the push the clutch in here and shift gears. Along with Buddhism and spiritual well-being, I am going to share with you something else I find fascinating. I have always been intrigued by the number 13. Along with 3 and 7... 13 is one of my favorite numbers. For a long time... 137 has been my favorite number. It's got all the numbers I like. I'm also fond of 1137. "Eleven thirty-seven" has a snappy cadence to it.

I like the number 13. When I was 12, I broke a mirror on Friday the 13th. Without skipping a beat, my Dad said, "Dana, this means you get 7 years *good* luck!" Cool. This is a striking memory for me. My father was not often inclined to reach out and say something fun to Dana.

The number 13 also had its effect on the date Scott and I got married. His parents got married on June 13th. Scott has tender childhood memories of his mom being sad… and his dad in the doghouse… because Dad forgot their wedding anniversary. Again. Scott decided he would nip that one right in the bud.

He proposed to me. I said "Yes." Scott's next words were, "Okay, we've got to get married on a national holiday." Thus guaranteeing he wouldn't forget our anniversary. We got married on the 4th of July. Which, it turns out, is a terrific anniversary date.

I was *muy* intrigued as I began to grok… some people have "a thing" about the number 13. A fear of black cats… don't walk under ladders… kinda "thing." For some folks, this is much more of a *megillah* than I could have ever imagined. This discomfort… this avoidance of using 13… is so well-established, there's even a word for it. *Triskaidekaphobia*… fear of the number 13.

President Franklin Roosevelt was uncomfortable with the number 13. He had a secretary who was always on call for state dinners and other functions... just in case the awkward 13 people turned up. FDR's secretary would be invited to join the event or dinner party to make the 14th guest.

Some buildings do not have a 13th floor. Many elevators have no #13 button to push. Which has always struck me as kind of self-delusional. "Let's just pretend it's not there."

Not to be forgotten... Apollo 13... the ill-fated, 7th manned mission in the Apollo space program. The 3rd spaceship intended to land on the Moon. Things did not go well. There were mishaps. A movie was made.

As with most superstitions... people are uncomfortable with the number 13... and Friday the 13th... for its own sake. Without any need for rationale nor pertinent background information.

Fascinatingly... there's plenty of pertinent background info to be had. Thirteen is significant to Christians because it is the number of people who were present at the Last Supper... Jesus and his 12 disciples. During medieval times... the story of the Last Supper was amended to cast Judas... the apostle who betrayed Jesus... as the 13th member of the party to arrive.

There are some who trace the infamy of the number 13 back to ancient Norse culture. In Norse mythology... the beloved hero Balder was killed at a banquet by that troublesome god Loki. Evidently, Loki crashed the party of twelve... bringing the number of celebrants to... you guessed it... 13.

This Norse banquet story... as well as the narrative of the Last Supper... led to one of the most entrenched 13-related beliefs: Never sit down to a meal in a group of 13 people. Maybe FDR knew more than I'm giving him credit for.

There is an alternative weekly newspaper called *The Chicago Reader* which is published in... wait for it... Chicago. Founded in 1971, *The Reader*... as it is known to its friends... is popular for its literary style, coverage of the arts, and creative nonfiction. A popular question-and-answer column... "The Straight Dope"... has been published in *The Reader* since 1973.

The "World's Smartest Human"... Cecil Adams (most likely a pseudonym)... is designated as the column's author. Cecil responds to often-unusual inquiries with humor... and at times, exhaustive research into obscure and arcane issues. Urban legends, history, science... old wives tales, inventions, and the like. This column is syndicated in more than 30 newspapers in the U.S. and Canada.

"The Straight Dope" appears under the tag-line: "Fighting ignorance since 1973 (it's taking longer than we thought)."

Relevant to our current conversation about the number 13... here is an exchange between a reader and Cecil himself:

Dear Cecil:

Currently 13 is considered to be an unlucky number. However, I am told it used to be — and in some earth-worshiping, i.e., pagan, religions still is — a lucky and magical number. Consequently, there were 13 months and 13 zodiac signs (the Gemini twins had separate identities). Knowing how Christianity and other god-as-a-man-based religions were prone to say that what the pagans (Earth-and-god-as-a-woman) considered good was bad, I wonder if this was the case with the number 13. And why was 13 singled out of an infinity of numbers in the first place? Also, if the number 13 is so bad, why is it reflected so many times on the U.S. $1 bill — 13 levels in the pyramid, 13 stars, 13 arrows, 13 stripes, 13 leaves, and 13 olives? Is it because of the original 13 colonies? ~ L.S. Thomas, Berkeley, California

Cecil replies:

Thirteen stripes, 13 colonies ... nah, it's just coincidence. The matter of how 13 came to be a numerological pariah, on the other hand, is an interesting story. While your rap about the pagans is a little off the wall (Thor the feminist?), you're right about one thing: 13 hasn't always been considered unlucky.

Though I wasn't able to do as thorough a study of cross-cultural number significance as I would have liked — the Straight Dope Field Survey Team preferred to be read to from *The Cat in the Hat* — what I've seen suggests that in ancient times 13 either was considered in a positive light or, more commonly, wasn't considered at all. I note, for example, that the Gnostics of the early Christian era totted up 13 Conformations of the Holy Beard. The significance of the Holy Beard is not entirely clear to me, but I gather it's something you wanted on your side. Thirteen was also once associated with the Epiphany by mainstream Christians, the Christ child having received the Magi on his thirteenth day of life.

But 13's stock dropped like a rock in the Middle Ages. The proximate cause of this, apparently, was the observation that Judas, the betrayer of Jesus, made 13 at the table. Other great medieval minds, I read here, pointed out that "the Jews murmured 13 times against God in the exodus from Egypt, that the thirteenth Psalm concerns wickedness and corruption, that the circumcision of Israel occurred in the thirteenth year," and so on.

Pretty thin excuse for maligning a number that never meant any harm, you may think. I agree. We must inquire further, and if we do, we conclude that while open hostility to 13 may be relatively recent, folks have had their suspicions about it for quite a while. Thirteen is a prime; primes have always attracted attention (compare 7). What's worse, 13 is one past 12, the dozen, almost universally regarded as a perfect number, signifying harmony and all things good. Thirteen, by contrast, is a number of transgression, taking matters one step too far, turning harmony into discord.

A bit of a stretch? Maybe. But consider how often 13s seem to intrude on our tidy arrangements of 12. In many a twelvemonth, to use an old term, there are 13 full moons, and a woman on a 28-day menstrual cycle will be "unclean," as Leviticus puts it, 13 times a year. The moon has long been a female symbol, and the full moon, (male) chroniclers tell us, is when (female) witches fly. I hesitate on that evidence alone to ascribe triskaidekaphobia to the fell hand of the patriarchy. But 13's bad reputation may have more to do with fear of women, witchcraft, and disorder than is commonly supposed.

~ Cecil Adams

Pretty interesting... and extensive... eh? So's you know... archive columns of both "The Straight Dope" and *The Chicago Reader* are available online.

Personally, remembering elementary school American history lessons... I *do* believe all of those 13s appearing on the U.S. $1 bill... and the 13 red and white stripes on the U.S. Flag... *are* a shout-out to the original 13 colonies. Maybe Cecil was joking us about that.

※ ※ ※

In my late teens... this scenario began showing up in my head. It is a significant component of my inner journey... and has popped up many times.

I am in a large, outdoor sports arena packed with people. The stands are full and there is standing room only as people fill the playing field.

I have 2 perspectives in this visual.

In one... I am standing on the field, behind a man's right shoulder. He has a suit jacket on. I am shorter than he is. I am looking around his upper right arm at a raised platform set up on the field with several people standing on it.

Simultaneously... I am one of the people on that raised platform. I am standing in front of the others, looking out at this mass of people.

Telepathically, I say to the people assembled...

> "You are hearing me inside your own head.
> Lift your consciousness as high as you can,
> as fast as you can."

Then something happens.

I don't know what.

I have always felt this scenario occurs in this Life.

I'm sure it's not a past Life. It could be a future incarnation.

The take-away being...

> "Lift your consciousness as high as you can,
> as fast as you can."

This strikes me as a good idea.

I knew you'd want to know.

Now let's revisit The Nature of The Soul. Over the years... I've had most intriguing experiences rereading that mind-expanding material. Offered thru-out the teachings are many tools... techniques... invocations and meditations. Some of these tools I have chosen to work with... some I have not. As I reread the material... I come to pages with techniques I have not explored or utilized... and they are merely words on paper. As I come to pages with tools and meditations I have explored and made good use of... those pages are alive! The words themselves are dimensional...

full of meaning... a wealth of insight. So far beyond words printed on a page. They zing!

The following 4 stanzas are written at the very end of The Nature of The Soul. The final comment. I have "exercised" these phrases countless time... both in my personal meditation and with groups. I call them to mind as I am cruising thru Life... riding on a bus... waiting somewhere for something... before I go to sleep at night. All to sweet reward. It is an honor to share them with you.

> Dare to drop your conflict.
> Dare to become filled with Love.
> Dare to stop all thought and receive the Spirit of God.
> Dare to take the step...
> With the eye lifted... away from the chasm...
> fastened upon the Light.

Each line = a gymnasium of state-of-the-art awareness exercise equipment.

Many times... I start with the first line and "exercise" it until I feel I truly *have* "dropped my conflict." That, in and of itself, is a feat. Well worth the effort. *Well* worth the exercise.

Truly, if you're going to teach yourself anything... teach yourself to drop your conflict. Yes, I know. Our conflict can be wildly persuasive. Wanting us to know it is *so* important.

Dare To Take The Step

But, here's a clue... let's call our inner conflict what it is... Major Distraction. Fussity fuss fuss.

Your inner conflict is never the ally it pretends to be.

Then, after dropping my conflict (as best I can), I move on to exercising "Become *filled* with Love." As you can well-imagine, this is also a practice I highly recommend. A real game-changer. What does it feel like to be *filled with Love*? I clearly remember the first time it happened in me. Whoa. "It's really happening!" Truly sublime. Definitely something you want to explore. Find out for yourself.

"Stop all thought"... always a meaningful endeavor. Exercise *that* muscle.

"Receive the Spirit of God" brings its own peace-full stillness. Key word... *receive*.

And that last line... "Dare to take the step"... applies to so many different Life aspects and possibilities. Yes... *that* step. "With the eye lifted"... always a helpful reminder. "Away from the chasm"... oh that crazy chasm... self-doubt... worry... fear of... countless self-inflicted limitations. Reorient. Recalibrate. As you "fasten upon the Light." A mighty tool. Simultaneously lifting and deepening. Well worth exploring. And exercising.

Exercise your awareness equipment. Work *those* muscles. Have at it.

Several times, reading this book, you've seen me mention… "We are Spirit living a human experience." In the 1980s, as I first became aware of this phrase… this concept gracefully put into words by the French philosopher, Pierre Teilhard de Chardin… I thought, "That's perfect. That says it!"

Living from 1881 until 1955… Teilhard de Chardin was a Jesuit priest. He was also a trained paleontologist and geologist. A well-rounded guy. He was known for his synthesis of science and theology. Blending these 2 orientations… integrating them with his fervent belief in the theory of evolution… got him into hot water with the Catholic Church. Much of his writing was banned by the Church during his lifetime… and after.

In this case, his actual words were:

> "You are not a human being
> in search of a spiritual experience.
> You are a spiritual being
> immersed in a human experience."

"Immersed." Engrossed. Absorbed. Occupied. Captivated. I'll say!

Years ago… as I was researching what Teilhard said… and the way he said it… I came across another quote of his which resonates deeply with me:

> "Some day...
> after we have mastered the winds,
> the waves, the tides and gravity...
> we shall harness for God the energies of love.
> And then, for the second time in the history of the world...
> man will have discovered fire."

Well spoke. Worth pondering.

"We shall harness for God the energies of love"... within the hearts and minds of Humankind. It's all an inside job. Inside each of us. The Pivotal 4th Kingdom shall know its rightful place within the scope of the Planetary Life. We will have, indeed, "discovered fire"... on a whole other expanded level. Human awareness dimensionalized. Ignited by love.

This whole other expanded, dimensional level makes me think of the further unfolding of Maylaigh. Earlier... telling the story of how this word came to be... I mentioned the "phases" of The Love That Heals. The "evolving steps" in human awareness development... as they began to reveal themselves in the early '90s. Pre-Maylaigh. Maylaigh. Uber Maylaigh.

Pre-Maylaigh: The Love That Feels. Before a person can really delve into "healing" love... one has to touch into "feeling" love. You have to be willing to access yourself emotionally. Self-kindness = always a worthy companion to bring along on this safari into the vast and wide jungle of your emotional nature.

I have mentioned once or thrice... so many folks are terrified by their emotions. Paralyzed as they consider their feelings. Just as, in my late teens and thru my 20s, I had been afraid I would find out something(s) about my emotional self that would "make me go insane" (whatever I meant by that). Many people are reluctant to explore their emotional self. Afraid of what they may find there. How *bad* it will be.

So, let me ask you this... do you thirst for greater meaning in your Life? For a sense of purpose? For greater inner understanding? Greater peace? Do you feel "something" is missing? "Inside I feel miserable most of the time. Is this what Life is all about?"

Have you gotten to the point where you're thinking... "Why does this all hurt so much?" "Is this all there is?"

The answer to that last question would be... no.

Here is where the work begins. Or... attitude being everything... you could say, here's where the *fun* begins.

Consciously or unconsciously... "religious" or otherwise... we are all looking for Refreshment of The Spirit.

Your thirst for greater meaning can be a weary yearning... a pain that leadens your heart. Or... this innate longing can be the impetus to spur you on. To delve and explore within. To experience a Life of meaning and substance. To find happiness. Peace. Joy.

And thus... The Love That Feels. Pre-Maylaigh becomes your inner process... as you move from wanting more... to allowing more... receiving more... appreciating more.

I also mention getting "whacked" by Life. It seems each of us trips over our Threshold of Awakening thru an emotionally traumatic experience. Often involving some degree of loss.

We each reside in a place of inner pain. Inner turmoil. We each carry a heavy burden. Always anticipating confrontation. Chronically. We live our lives steeped in unconscious fear of reprisal and retaliation.

We cloud our current vision as we continue to hope... somehow... the past could be different.

Beginning to wake up... the first thing we meet is... struggle... pain... fear. The artifice of The Great Captivator. The Great Ruse. As the awakening process begins to stir... all the "it's not fair" we hold inside churns and roils to the surface of our awareness. Like molten lava.

But, you know what? Here's a different perspective to consider when confronting the owies... the difficulties and challenges which manifest as troubling experiences in your Life. These very strains and struggles are actually revealing tender places inside you... showing up *for you to love*.

Truly.

Turn to the places in yourself that feel... slighted... anxious... unworthy... angry... and simply love them. As these aspects of you show up... they cry out for your attentive caring. Use your imagination yoga... pour love into and thru-out these hurting, vulnerable, apprehensive aspects of yourself.

Simply love them.

Our fixation with finding fault... it's *my* fault... it's *his* fault...it's *their* fault... vs. embracing response-ability. This is *my* responsibility.

I *get to* do this versus I *have to* do this.

That one inner shift turns your Life around. "I have to do the dishes." Grumble, grumble. Fuss... vs... "I get to do the dishes." Gratitude that we have dishes, and enough food... enough friends and family... enough good times... that there are dishes to do.

I *get* to rather than I *have* to = a miniscule, yet profound, inner modification. Shift happens.

Traveling thru your Life... rather than failure and bitterness... recognize "I have more to learn." Rather than discouragement and beating yourself up... "I have more to learn." Rather than blame and shame... "I have more to learn."

Find a new way around your pain. Insist on engaging the lesson.

"What am I to learn here?" You begin to see and dismantle your inner obstacles. As I commented earlier... you remove the stones from your inner walls and resistance. You reconfigure. The stones from your inner obstacles become the road you build to your own knowing. To clear vision. To release from self-imposed limitation.

The choices you make... what you learn... becomes your path to wholeness.

Early in my relationship with Scott... a difficulty I was dealing with led to this phrase appearing in my head:

> I trust the Light of the Soul
> to reveal what I am to learn.

Ohhh, I thought at the time. *Good one.*

As with so many concepts and phrases, I would pull this one out now and again to contemplate. A year or more went by. One day... looking at this "friendly reminder" again... more Light appeared. This insightful phrase unfolded itself this way:

I trust the Light of the Soul to reveal what I am to learn.
 I trust the Light of the Soul to reveal what I am.
  I trust the Light of the Soul to reveal.
   I trust the Light of the Soul.
    I trust the Light.
     I trust.

This "exercise"... this journey... takes you to A Deep and Certain Peace Within. Trust is a powerful ally. Bring it along with you on your inner trek. Trust is a helpful compadre as you peruse and ponder... what is this fear... this resistance I have to my own self-exploration?

So's you know... you don't have to analyze and "figure this out." You *can* just step over your resistance... your hesitation inside. And proceed.

Without making the choice to become more self-aware... you're stuck. Bewildered and perplexed as you toil within your own emotional reactions and mis-beliefs. Imprisoned. Victimized by your own self-imposed... self-inflicted... limitations.

Alan Cohen... a present-day inspirational speaker and award-winning author... shares insight into this self-enlightening process. "At some point the spiritual path rises beyond form like an airplane rises beyond a runway. Practices are prelude. Do them until they lift you beyond them."

Lifting beyond them. The Love That Feels = you, allowing layers of armor to crumble away from your heart. You... gently applying Love within your own fine self. You... beginning to use the stuff of your everyday world... the joys and the sorrows... to awaken within your inner Life.

Lifting beyond.

The first steps to Awareness Liberation are the steps you choose to take into and thru your pain. The places in yourself you resist and deny the most... these are the places holding the key to unlock you within yourself.

You hold all the keys.

You hold all the locks.

I know it seems like the locks are holding... shackling... you. Another of Life's obstacle illusions.

You create your own reality... by what you call what you experience. How you explain your experience to yourself. How you recollect it when it comes up again. Your story.

The way you feel inside yourself makes your Life what it is. You really are the only person who can heal yourself. You are the only person who can help yourself. You are the only person who can make yourself grow.

Even if you are seeing a good therapist... you are the one doing the work. When you visit a healer... you are the one allowing the energy to have its healing effect within your bodies.

Your pain looks and feels completely different when you see it from a different perspective. A changed perspective.

Stop looking "out there" for your reason to be happy. Or as the source of your pain.

If not you... who?

If not now... when?

From the vantage point of a changed inner perspective… your Life transforms. Unanticipated panoramas open before you.

Here is a "changed perspective"… an "unanticipated panorama":

Imagine your Higher Self is delighted with you.

Imagine… your Higher Self judging you… not for all the things you have done wrong… but for all of the things you are doing right.

Good job, You!

Imagination yoga. Attitude adjustment. Emotions stretching. Recalibrating.

Be willing to gently turn to your emotional self… to see what's there. To feel. It is a mighty exploration. It only looks scary before you begin.

You just need to get your footing. Once you gain a certain familiarity… once you trust yourself and your Life even a little bit … once you are actually moving around in your emotional self… it's all quite engaging. Fascinating. Worthwhile.

The fear and uncertainty we feel around our emotions are just a ruse. A sly maneuver on the part of The Great Captivator. The Great Concealer. Keeping us concealed. From ourselves. Obscured. Hidden. From our own awakening.

Dare To Take The Step

Fear of our emotions is an artifice. It would be a joke... except it's so not funny. Emotional pain and turmoil... and our fear of that... keeps us stewing in anxiety and concern. Uncertain of our own self-worth.

Artifice, be gone!

Don't let the scary stuff... the scared you... win. That's not who you truly are. As John Lennon would say... "That's just a pig's foot of your imagination."

Step over the scaredy places inside. Be kind to your fine self. Strap on the old pith helmet and begin excavating. Dig around. Bring the Light in. A safari of the heart. More Light. Light in the places inside yourself that are dark and doubting.

Bring Light into your troubled heartache. Sit with Light. Sit in Light. Allow the Light to *be*. To gently reveal. Allow the Light to gently reveal yourself to you.

Release yourself from self-blame. From self-neglect. Release yourself from over analyzing. Release yourself from scraping off old emotional scabs... revisiting past slights and hurts. They feel so real... so fresh. Each time. Ow.

Release yourself from rehashing the anguish... the embarrassment... the hurt... sharp and fresh as if it happened this morning. Be kind to yourself. Entertain the notion... you can change. You *can* alter... guide... evolve... your responses to your Life. Gently open to The Love That Feels.

Don't look back... that's not the way we're going.

Continue to breathe.

Once you allow yourself to explore The Love That Feels... The Love That Heals feels more accessible. Ahhhh... healing. Becoming. Bringing yourself out of self-doubt. Pessimism. Despair. Opening to the possibilities of your own goodness.

Truly. Your. Own. Goodness.

Within yourself... move from doubt and apathy... to awakening awareness. Healing. Awake. Aware. Alive.

Alive within the living of your Life. Alive with the reality of new possibilities. Alive with certainty. "I can *do* this!"

Transformation times.

> The Love That Heals is an opportunity for you
> to open your heart...
> open your mind...
> open your identity...
> in a whole, new way.

To the healing... joyful... transforming power of Love.

A portal opens inside you. The Truth of Love... a palpable... innate... thriving force... pours forth. Allowing you to look upon your world and see... the joy... the good... the worthiness. The gentle perfection. That is always here. Seen... found... as you look for it.

You nourish *those* aspects of Life. Calling them forth. As you give your attention to them.

When you open to Love... as a transforming force within your consciousness... you do yourself A Big Favor.

Open to your true self. Love comes out to greet you. Welcome home.

We live in a world that rarely allows itself to see or know the truth of the power of Love. Just as intuition is poo-pooed... seen as lesser than intellecting. So, too, Love is tagged as "Pollyanna"... unrealistic... sappy. Ahhh... tho folks may pontificate in that direction... they know not of what they speak. Ignorance prevails. We humans continue stagnating in our own despair.

As you begin to transform... it may take you some time to find your equilibrium. It serves you well to remember... the reason you are incarnate in human form is to become more aware... more awake.

To remember you *are* Love.

Growing beyond... knowing beyond... limitations and false beliefs. It becomes increasingly clear... Love heals your inner terror. Your inner pain. Cutting thru the inner fog and mumbo jumbo. The Healing Power of Love brings you to a place of clarity and realization.

Open to your spiritual self... in the way that makes sense to you. Explore.

Spiritual reality reveals itself to you in
ways you could never imagine.
You are revealed to you in ways you could never imagine.

Let's check out the benefits of being more awake and aware within The Love That Heals:

1. A loving familiarity with your emotional self allows you to enjoy walking your Path... feeling vibrant and alive within the process of your Life.
2. You are able to choose which energies are going to find expression thru you.
3. You get to know yourself better. Your responses. Who you are. How you are.
4. You can consciously apply yourself to your Life. You are now in your Life more effectively.
5. You understand yourself... and Life... more dimensionally.
6. You sprout wings... as you give yourself the freedom of release from struggle.
7. No longer blinded by your own inner shackles... you are free from... concern... worry... self-inflicted limitations.
8. You are more available to help and lift others... with clarity and compassion.

The Love That Heals is the bridge between the 4th Kingdom of Human Awareness and the 5th Kingdom of Soul Consciousness. The Love That Heals is an evolutionary force... moving humanness beyond Intellect to Intuition and Instantaneous Knowing. To Inspiration.

Your quest for greater awareness is a quest for Love.

Refreshment of The Spirit = Love.

If you are not experiencing Love outside you... take the time to consciously experience Love inside you. This is your work. Your choice. Don't wait for "somebody else" to Love you. This is yours to do.

Get crackin.'

Trust Love to flourish your Life. Release yourself from fearing God. God has no interest in punishing you nor demonstrating harsh disfavor. God is up to many more favorable endeavors.

You exercise Love. You consciously bring Love in again and again. And again. Into yourself. Into your perceptions. Your expression. Your relationships. You bring Love into the situations and circumstances in your world.

As you practice... calcification dissolves. You transform your emotional nature. To become the Light-Reflective Surface for the Light of The Soul it is intended to be. The Light-Reflective Surface it is longing to be.

You are the one who allows... this luminous realization... this transforming power of The Love That Heals... to be active in your life. Make room inside yourself. Inside your self-identity. You are the only one who can give yourself this gift.

> The Love That Heals...
> Restores the Heart...
> Inspires the Mind...
> Quickens the Awareness.

You are Spirit coming alive in Matter.

Uber Maylaigh. Ultra. Stellar. The Love That Heals... above and beyond. More than healing. What you do and where your Life goes when you are exercising Healing Love. When you are whole. Awake.

Who are you *now*... in this new context?

I've said before... "Intellect is not the final gate." Emotional healing is not the final gate. There is so much more fun to be had. So much more to do. To be. To actualize.

Uber Maylaigh... The Love That Reveals. Reveals what? Reveals so much more of who we humans are. And what we're here to do. Reveals more of who *you* are. More of what you are here to do. To be.

Offering you further joyous dance steps in the Tango of Life.

The Love That Reveals creates a conscious alignment. Substantiating an invocative channel... for inpouring uplifting energies. Light. Love. The Will-to-Good.

A peaceful certainty. Your perspective evolves. By its very nature... this certainty invites you to contribute to the world around you in a constructive, uplifting way. In light of this rich context... you recognize your aspiration to connect with Higher Awareness for what it is. An experience and expression of Greater Love.

Your frame of reference dimensionalizes. You look at and experience your Life from a different vista. A different perspective. Does the scenery change? Or is it you?

The Love That Reveals offers Deepening of The Spirit. Deepening your experience of your Life... what you believe Life to be. Deepening into yourself. Joy. Knowing. Fulfillment. You find Greater Richness in the living of your Life.

This Force of Uplifting Love transforms your conscious awareness. Your weary heart is refreshed... vitalized.

Clarity. Insight. Certainty. A gift. To you. Within the very living of this Life of yours. In ways you could only hope would be possible.

> You do not transform to become someone else.
> You transform to become who you truly are.

The Sheer Joy of the human incarnate experience = you, getting to be a redemptive dynamic. Exploring the contours of clear vision. Cleansing and reclaiming human awareness for the Forces of Love. "I *get* to do this!"

Stretching your identity... your mind... your heart. You embody and outpicture soul-conscious awareness. By being your Self.

The generations behind us and the generations before us are pulling for your enlightened awareness. Promoting. Advocating. Assisting. You.

> Living... as we do... within a stream
> of ever-evolving awareness,
> We are all in this together.
> Focusing on soul conscious awareness.
> Focusing on becoming a soul conscious incarnate.
> Focusing on bringing soul awareness
> more actively into daily awareness.
>
> Soul Awareness.
> Compassion. Understanding. Forgiveness. Service.
> Knowing you are capable of these states of being.
> Knowing you are capable of acting and
> responding to Life in this way.
>
> Your heart overflows with gratitude.
>
> Inshallah.

Becoming an instrument of The Love That Heals... The Love That Reveals:

1. Great-fullness radiates in your heart.
2. Your past and your future are transformed.
3. You become a channel for Good as never before.
4. The Hand of The Great Creator works thru you.
5. You grace our world with the artistry of your life.

Your unique spirit is what makes you... you. Your unique spirit makes your Life... *your* Life. The human experience gives meaning to existence. Your contributions to Life... your challenges... your successes... your realizations... give Life substance and value.

The very uniqueness of you... your talents... your gifts... your capabilities... are noticed and appreciated by Life.

Embrace the likelihood of your success.

Beauty surrounds you in your journey ahead.
Happiness is your companion.
Your finest vision will be fulfilled.

Love is the final gate.

Several years ago... while guiding a group meditation... insightful inspiration occurred to me which had never entered my mind before. I love when that happens.

I share this remarkable tool of transformation with you here.

At some point in your meditation... or as you are preparing to go to sleep at night... generate positive energy in your thoughts and feelings. "Golden Light" is always my go-to. Use whichever phrase or image resonates with you. I will use "Golden Light" as I describe this astoundingly effective way to integrate your awareness.

As you are generating this positive, glowing, Golden Light energy... feel yourself centered in your heart.

Visualizing... using your Imagination Yoga... think of yourself as you were yesterday morning. Seeing yourself... send Golden Light back to yourself then. In your heart and mind... travel back to yourself 5 years ago. See a mental picture of yourself then. Pour Golden Light to your "5 years ago" self. Travel back to yourself as a young adult... pour Golden Light to yourself as you were then. Take your time. No need to rush. Pour Golden Light to your teenage self. Pour Golden Light into and thru-out your teen years. Remember yourself as a child. Pour Golden Light to your child self. Your baby self. See yourself on the day you were born.

Silently or aloud... sound the ancient, sacred OM. Pour this Golden Light to yourself as you drew your very first breath in this incarnation. As your newborn self, receive this Golden Light. Give yourself a few moments here. At this threshold. Your arrival in this Life.

As you consciously bring Love Light Awareness to your new born self... your child self... your teenage self... your young adult self... you are healing the fabric of time. Evolving the tapestry of your Life. With Grace.

Bring your awareness to your present Life. Pour Golden Light before you along your vibrant, alive Path. Pour this Light into your relationships... your current challenges... your joys... your work... your creative expression.

Sound the OM as you consciously direct Golden Light along your Path and into your Life as it is now. Allow yourself a few moments to sit... to be... in your Golden Light present.

Consider yourself as you are waking up tomorrow. Send Golden Light to your tomorrow self. Pour Golden Light into your future as it unfolds before you. Intentionally. Consider the friendships which are yet to come. Greet them with Golden Light. Consider your future plans and endeavors... those you know about... and those still to be revealed. Pour Golden Light into your future self... into your future Life.

As you sound the OM... pour this Golden Light to yourself as you draw your very last breath in this incarnation. As you cross that threshold. Your departure.

Give yourself a moment. Or 3. Perhaps 10. Savor.

Allow your attention to relax.

You have blessed and elevated the underlying fabric of your Life... as you consciously send this positive, Golden Light energy to... your past self... your present... your future. You have lifted the very intent... the energy dynamic... the livingness... of all the interweaving cords and threads of your past, present, and future Life. Enlivening the tapestry of your Life.

We live within a streaming continuity of consciousness. Just because you may not feel this... or have never considered it... does not mean this is not true. You have a positive influence within the recollecting of your Life. You have a positive effect on the foundation of your Life by sending positive energy "back" to yourself.

You lift your present... you engage and nourish positive factors... as you consciously send vibrant, reliable energy along your Path and into your Life as it is now. You bless your own Life... and its effect in your world... as you exercise self-kindness and clear vision. As you acknowledge and appreciate the many and varied miracles, blessings, and connexions weaving thru-out the tapestry of your Life. As you invigorate all the varied ways... the different ways... miracles, blessings, and connexions show up.

Pouring Golden Light and positive energy into your future... you set in motion an avalanche of Good. Positive forces are directed toward prospering your own well-being. See your future footsteps outlined with sparkling Golden Light… furthering you along your path. Clearly showing you the way. To serve. To continue contributing to well-being.

You lift and ground the continuing unfolding of your own Life expression.

It is essential to realize… we humans are part of a vast lineage of good.

There have been beings of Light… compassion… insight… clarity… thru-out human history. Such aware, compassionate humans are alive all over the world today. Present company included.

I see you.

As you consider these beings of transforming awareness and Light… you may recall… early in *Holy Wow!* I acknowledged Albert Einstein, and shared his insight:

> "There are only two ways to live your Life.
> One is as though nothing is a miracle.
> The other is as thought everything is a miracle."

As we draw to a close… I again call upon this amazing being and his ever-perceptive words:

> "Strange is our situation here upon earth. Each of us comes for a short visit, not knowing why, yet sometimes

seeming to a divine purpose. From the standpoint of daily life, however, there is one thing we do know: That we are here for the sake of others... above all for those upon whose smile and well-being our own happiness depends, for the countless unknown souls with whose fate we are connected by a bond of sympathy. Many times a day, I realize how much my outer and inner life is built upon the labors of people, both living and dead, and how earnestly I must exert myself in order to give in return as much as I have received and am still receiving."

"I realize how much my outer and inner life is built upon the labors of people, both living and dead"... this continuity of consciousness we are all part of.

The vibrant flow of Life awareness streaming behind us. Our foundation. Those we have come from. Our ancestors. Ancestors of our family lineage. Ancestors of our spiritual lineage. Our tribe. The vitality of Life as it streams exuberantly before and beyond us. Those who are coming. The ones our current choices and actions support and bond with... as Life continues unfolding after our time here is done.

Numerous beings of clarity and Light are coming to follow us in the future. What we do now... each individual choice... contributes to that lineage of Good. Encouraging present-day forces which uplift well-being... in fact fosters

the lightworkers of the future. You are an intrinsic strand…
as this ever-unfolding tapestry of Light weaves on.

As your awareness continues to expand… you don't just get "there"… and you're "there." And "this" is "all over." Once you get "there"… you are completely clear… this isn't about you. It never has been.

You don't clarify yourself to yourself and then go on a spree of total self-indulgence in the realm of "all about me." The more clear you are inside yourself… the more clearly you see… you are here to help others. You serve God by serving others. Not by wearing certain clothes or eating certain foods… certainly not by proselytizing. Nor judging. But by helping make Life better for others.

To again quote Cory Booker… "I'm not as interested in what you have to tell or sell… as in how you choose to live and give." Let's help each other out here.

Rabindranath Tagore (1861–1941)… known as The Bard of Bengal… a renowned poet, musician, author, and artist. Truly a Renaissance man. His words beautifully affirm this embrace of service to others. This embrace of service to Life.

> "I slept and dreamt that life was joy.
> I awoke and saw that life was service.
> I acted and behold!
> Service was joy!"

The choices you make within yourself strengthen this transforming power of healing Love within you. Within our world. As you encourage those around you in the living of their Life... as you let your own light shine... you do, in fact, give other people permission to do the same.

Clearly knowing yourself as an instrument of Light... a being of Spirit... you add one more grain of sand to the scales that hold the balance for our global future. Come a certain point... one grain of sand *will* tip the scale.

You... right now... may be that grain of sand.

On the list of Things To Do for this incarnation... let's see... oh, yes, here it is: Shine a Light to brighten the darkness of the time we live in. Check.

Today... allow yourself to be aided... guided... by those who have gone before you. Just as the mighty oak springs from the growth pattern in the tiny acorn... your full flowering is rooted in all who have been present here on Earth before you. Celebrate this continuity of Life.

Like a water molecule in the mighty ocean... I am part of a larger whole... great streaming Conscious Awareness. This whole is part of me.

Everyone who has done you a kind deed had a kind deed done for them. Every person who taught you something meaningful... had their own significant teachers, who imparted knowledge and wisdom to them.

Your mentors had mentors. Your teachers had teachers. Your grandmothers had grandmothers. Your sons will have grandsons. Your great-granddaughters will have granddaughters.

Feel this continuity of uplifting human consciousness as it flows thru you... thru your veins... your breath... your neural synapses. Thru your awareness... your abilities... your temperament.

Any choice you make today casts its impression on the instruments of Love coming in the future. Allow your heart to beat with the heartbeat of conscious awareness. Feel this Pulse of Life flowing thru you.

The Path *Is* The Goal.

May the blessings of Love rest upon you.
May Love's peace abide with you.
May Love's presence illuminate your heart.
Now and forever more.

Acknowledgments

With a warm heart, I acknowledge…

My awesome husband, Scott. Even after 37 years, you continue to delight me with your keen insight, your playful laughter, and your loving encouragement and support.

Our dear friend, Joy Utz, C.F.o.F. Our very own Certified Facilitator of Fun. Mahalo for you… and for your kind generosity and attentive, caring ways.

Rita Leiphart, C.C.H. Your artistry as a hypnotherapist helped me actually birth *Holy Wow!* after a ridiculously long gestation.

Our brilliant son, Isaiah. Oh, how you grace my Life just by being your fine self.

Our talented son-in-law, Michael Bashan, for recording the intros and outros to all of my audiobooks in his very professional sounding voice.

I am blessed beyond measure by the many gifts of insight and connexion which have come my way thanks to the extraordinary friends and fellow humans who have touched my Life. Special appreciation to our longtime friends, Jim and Martha Fish and their family… and to John Randolph Price and his lovely wife, Jan. A grateful shout-out to Chris Allen… Celiane Milner and her daughter, Amber… Beatrice Rose and her daughter, Sarah… and to Mitch Evans. From my Unity of Beaverton days… Tori Padellford, Mary Huebner, Bruce and Toni Blue Spruce Rodgers, Rennie Maguire, Grace Muncie-Jarvis, Linda Waltmire, Ruby Gallagher, Anne Morey aka Cupcake, Rev. Maureen Haley and Rev. Ed Townley. In Southern California… Gilmore Rizzo and Bryan Miller, Ida Smith, Nancy Thompson, Noreen Bernier, Dianalee and Joan, Patricia Satorie Barnes, Diane Sternbach, Ron Zoboblish, Rev. Dr. Maureen Hoyt, Revs. Michael and Mary Beth Speer, Rev. Shelly Downes, Rev. Harry Morgan Moses. Here, in Hawaii… Carolyn and Richard Williams, Bettina Linke and family, Mark Morphew, Cathy Spitzenberger, Robin Bush, Dorothy and Mary Ellen, Maureen and Eric Langberg, Sarah and Jason McCarthy, Barrie Rose, Jude McAnesby, Beth Brandt, Johanna Tilbury, Minoo Elison, Charlie Anderson, Marcia Masters and Rebecca Clancy.

I warmly thank my dear friend, Karen Myer, who is the only person who has read *Holy Wow!* in its entirety. Your acknowledgment of its content and your encouraging ways fortified me onward.

Mahalo to Cheryl Valle of Surf City Images for my headshots and outstanding family portraits. And for being such a pleasure to work with.

Acknowledgments

If Holy Wow! were to have a Fairy Godmother… she would be Amy Collins. You hold this book in your hands right now thanks to her generosity of spirit and skillful coaching. A Big Thanks to Amy. Period. And to Amy's right hand woman, the Executive Director of New Shelves Books, Keri-Rae Barnum, who has helped me immeasurably. More appreciation to Amy for recommending my ideal editors, Pam Cangioli and Kim Jace, as well as my very talented graphic artist and cover designer, Mila… Miladinka Milic. Pam Cangioli led me to Ghislain Viau who has done an excellent job as my interior book designer.

To each of you for the part you played in bringing *Holy Wow!* into being… Mahalo Plenty!

Acknowledging that you, kind Reader, might be interested in connecting with any of these talented and very helpful individuals… here are their websites:

Rita Leiphart – www.districthypnosis.com

Amy Collins – www.newshelves.com

Keri-Rae Barnum – www.newshelves.com

Pam Cangioli – www.proofedtoperfection.com

Miladinka Milic – www.milagraphicartist.com

Ghislain Viau – www.creativepublishingdesign.com

Cheryl Valle – www.surfcityimages.com

About The Author

Blessed to share the rich gifts of mindfulness, Dana has been teaching others to meditate for over 40 years. Recognizing we are Spirit living a human experience, she is fascinated by the rich tapestry of Life… and the many gifts and possibilities available to every human.

It is Dana's delight to play the temple gongs, bells and tingsha that grace her guided meditations. She recognizes this as "a past Life thing." As Dana says… "The resonant tones of the gongs take you places mere words could never find."

She follows her own advice to "choose to be amused." And finds great pleasure in being a wordsmith. As an ordained transdenominational minister, Dana is a Celebrationist, creating Weddings, Memorial Services, and other Life-enhancing ceremony and ritual

Dana and her husband, Scott, live in Kona, Hawaii, ever in awe of the miraculous sunsets.

Holy Wow! Volume III is Dana's third book.

A Free Gift From Dana St.Claire

I trust you are enjoying reading Holy Wow!

Help other folks find this book.

Please write a review and post it at Goodreads.com or Amazon… at Barnes & Noble or on your own social media. Anywhere that strikes you as a good idea. You can use the same review on the different sites. Only a sentence or 2 is enough to let other readers know your experience of Holy Wow! and how you like it. (You can write more if you are so inspired.)

Much Appreciated.

Email me a copy of your review and where you posted to RevDanaStClaire@gmail.com.
I will send you a free MP3 with a special selection of tracks from my Guided Gong Meditation CDs.

Holy Wow!
The Handbook for Human Awareness Waking Up.

www.ingramcontent.com/pod-product-compliance
Lightning Source LLC
Chambersburg PA
CBHW031058080526
44587CB00011B/733